How to Develop Products and Sell Them Online

Start Your Own Online Business

Entrepreneur Series

John Davidson

Mendon Cottage Books

JD-Biz Publishing

Disclaimer

Read before you begin. These business ideas or plans are intended as a guide only! Read these instructions completely through once and understand what is required.

Our books are available at

1. Amazon.com

2. Barnes and Noble

3. Itunes

4. Kobo

5. Smashwords

6. Google Play Books

Download Free Books!
http://MendonCottageBooks.com

Table of Contents

Introduction

The world of eCommerce is grabbing more and more cyberspace, at lightning speed, than ever before. Online businesses are growing in big leaps and bounds. Selling online is increasingly becoming less of an option and more of a mandatory survival requirement. Online business empires are being created even by those who never thought of making a business worth a few hundred dollars. Looking at Forbes list of the top 10 richest people on this planet, you will realize that more than half of them are techpreneurs who have invested in the world of electronic technologies such as those presented by the marvels of the internet.

These days, you can hardly make your global presence be felt without the aid of the internet. Are you wondering how and where to start doing your business on the internet? This book is just the right key to opening that door to the limitless world of internet business. Don't dwarf yourself to extinction. Grab this opportunity now! Welcome.

We are right here for you. We see you and even before you dare knock, we've already laid out the red carpet for you. This book is a whole world of internet knowledge in itself. From this book, unlimited space awaits you to fill it with your adventurous entrepreneurial prowess. Territories await you in cyberspace for you to conquer and you will be king if you dare make that first move.

Once again, WELCOME!

How to Develop New Products

"DEVELOPING NEW PRODUCTS AND SELLING THEM ONLINE"

John Davidson

BATC - CBRC

Specialized Design Systems

SDSPlans.com   Product Development - Selling Online

Figure 2a Developing New Products

Eight Simple Steps for New Product Development:

Developing a new product does not mean you have to stay in the dark. There is an easier way. What you need is a clear map of how to achieve your idea. Indeed, developing a new product or service is only a small portion of the process of the complete journey which starts with ideas, producing them, to revealing the products in the market.

By following the steps set out, you can will have a more focused way to apply in the product development and these strategies can be applied for each different product and service development.

By implementing the following eight steps, you can develop your product and service online:

1. Idea Generation

Business is nothing but a group of ideas. That's why the improvement or the development of the products begins with some concepts. After generating the idea, in the next steps, the ideas are tested, one by one for their validity and reliability. So, at the beginning, all the concepts are regarded as the good concept. There is nothing wrong in providing a concept, whether that idea is good or bad.

 Ideas may come from various directions and experiences. The best way to assess an idea is by using SWOT analysis. SWOT stands for Strengths, Weaknesses, Opportunities and Threats, along with current market trends. This strategy can be used to illustrate the company's position and find out if its direction is in line with its business policy.

Along with these business research activities, the following methods should be used and these strategies will be in addition to your SWOT analysis:

- ❖ Perform market research

- ❖ Take suggestions from targeted customers, including feedback about your current products and their strengths and weaknesses

- ❖ Motivate employees and customers to provide suggestions

- ❖ Know about your competitors successes and failures

2. Idea Screening

This is considered as one of the most important steps to ensure that unsuitable ideas are eliminated as soon as possible. Concept will be looked at objectively, either by a group or a committee. In this stage, particular criteria should be maintained in regard to affordability and market possibilities. One should also give some thought to the possibility of product failure down the line even after certain investment.

3. Concept Development & Testing

After completing your screening stage, you need to ask the public about the product and look for opportunities in the market. You know that internal opinion is not as important, and that is why you should ask for outside opinions. Single out a small group of customers who can test your ideas so that you can understand their reactions, suggestions and any demands that may have. After completing this stage, the ideas should be used as the concept with enough in-depth customer's information so that the consumers can get complete idea about the product. And you should ask yourself, do they understand the idea? Is it something they would like to have?

From this stage you will get a second chance to develop your concept by using their feedback. At this time, you can again think about the marketing message, you can add some new ideas to your existing ideas, and do any modification that may be needed.

4. Business Analysis

After finalizing and testing the concept, the business policy will be assessed as to whether the new service or products will bring profit for the company. At this stage, you should have a detailed marketing policy, focusing on a particular market, and the position of the products. In the analysis, you should consider whether there is a demand for the products. There should also be a complete evaluation of the costs involved and an identification of the breakeven point, as well as comparisons done of other competitors' prices.

5. Product Development

When the production stage is approved, this will be done at a technical and marketing progress level. At this stage, only a limited production model will be created. This means that you can produce a product with your exact design through manufacturing. The positive thing is that you can test how the consumer feels about it and get the feedback on the design and quality, including the packaging.

6. Test Marketing

Test marketing is completely different from the ideas and consumer's feedback. It actually presents a model of the product to the proposed market as a whole, rather than just particular or specific elements. It is an important stage as it validates the entire concept for further modification of all the elements such as product, marketing strategy and the message which will be sent to the customers.

7. Commercialization

After initiating the concept, developing the idea and testing, the final steps need to be taken to go forward and to make preparations for its launch into the market. At this stage, you must finalize pricing and marketing plans, and the sales teams must be briefed about distribution so that the company can get ready for the finished stage.

8. Launch

At this stage, you need to have a detailed launching plan for the smooth presentation of the product to create maximum impact. In your launching plan, you should think about when, where and how you will launch the product and who will be your target consumer group. In the final stage, to avoid any future mistake, it's a good idea to get a review of the market performance in order to achieve the successful outcome of the products.

By following these simple stages, new products can be easily launched.

How to Sell Online

Developing products to sell online is not different from the usual process of developing offline products. However, it is the medium of selling them and the target market that makes a huge difference.

The product you develop must be in such a medium that it can be sold online. You can have digital products and non-digital products. Digital products, especially those that are non-tangible, are easy to sell online. Someone just needs to press the download button, pay up, and get the product. On the other hand, non-digital products, especially those that are tangible, would require an extra mode of delivery since the physical product must be delivered through physical means.

Why Sell on Amazon?

Figure 2b Amazon

Online stores such as Amazon and eBay have provisions for selling both tangible and non-tangible products. Amazon is specifically an important site to sell your physical products. You not only sell digital products, but also any tangible products such as clothing, footwear, household electronics, upholstery, jewelry, books, etc.

Amazon is an online store that is visited by millions of customers each day. It is a highly reputable brand that has customer trust. The biggest advantage of Amazon, over other stores, is the Amazon's FBA (Fulfillment by Amazon). Amazon's FBA is a facility that allows you to deliver your products to various physical stores available around the globe. Amazon will take care of everything ranging from branding, packaging, marketing, distributing, selling, and processing of financial transactions, on your behalf. Once you develop your product and deliver to Amazon's FBA center, everything is fulfilled! You can go on vacation, tour the world, or just take time off, and your account will continue make sales and you can withdraw your profits anywhere across the world.

Therefore, having such a facility right in your mind, while developing your product, could save you from a lot of stress and anxiety. They charge for the service, but it is a great way to test the market and get your sales going.

Whichever product you are developing, please know that digital accompaniments are inevitable! These digital accompaniments could be a product description video or eBook, Company description video or eBook, digital advertisement, software snippets, etc. You can never reap maximum benefits from your online business without digital accompaniments. What more? These accompaniments could be sellable products on their own! Thus, it is important to know how to create and market digital products. This is the reason why this book lays special emphasis on digital products.

Let's take an example of the author of this book who earns from holding training workshops and seminars. This is an intangible service, yet, he would need his training services to reach the widest market possible. How would he do it? That's the essence of this book.

WOULD THIS WORKSHOP SELL ONLINE?

- "Developing New Products and Selling Them Online"
- Developing ideas for new products
- How to put them online
- In-depth processes for launching a new product.
- Learn innovative methods for getting your product discovered; outsourcing tasks to get your product up faster; and not only staying ahead of the game, but being in charge of the game.

SDSPlans.com   Product Development - Selling Online

Figure 2c. Workshop

Fig.2c depicts some of the considerations one would make in selling a training workshop online. Yes, if you are a workshop trainer, you do not just end at the workshop door. You do not need to be just content with the workshop attendance fee, so look further down the horizon! Tap more income from the billions of people across the globe who are online each and every day.

WHAT WOULD THE PRODUCT LOOK LIKE

- MP4 Video Online Delivery
- DVD Delivery with Workbook
- Transcript turned into an ebook or Kindle
- Worksheets Handouts PowerPoint
- Automated Software Product

SDSPlans.com   Product Development - Selling Online

Figure 2d Product Outlook

Now that you have decided that you need to sell your product online, what would your product look like? Take the workshop as an example, as depicted by Fig.2d. There are various forms by which you can package your workshop product; MP4 Video for online delivery, DVD for physical delivery, transcribe your video into an eBook, transcribe your video into slide presentation, etc. Lastly, you can combine all the listed forms and transform them into automated software for downloads.

MP4 Video for Online Delivery

How do you create an MP4 video for online delivery? There are various ways by which you can create an MP4 video for online delivery. The most common of them all is to do video shooting of your event such as a workshop. Once video shooting is done, then you can use MP4 Video converters which are available online for free.

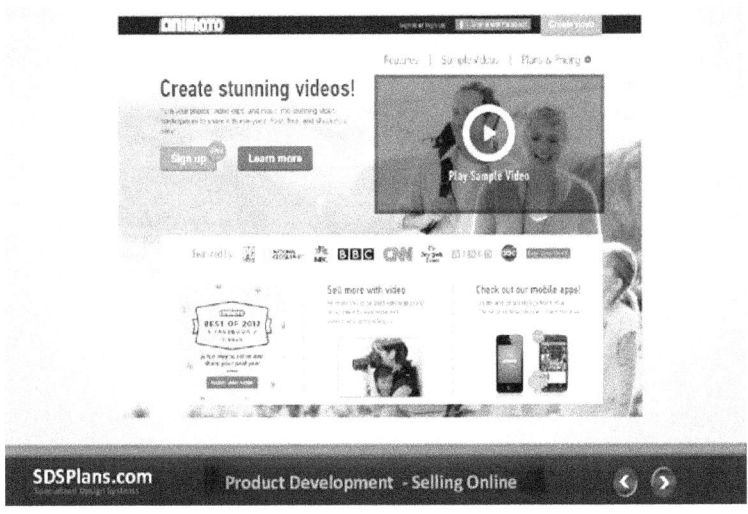

Figure 2e Animoto

The other way to create MP4 Video is to create a PowerPoint slideshow. Once you've created these slideshows, you upload them onto Animoto and they will be converted into videos. Animoto is a specialized online slides-to-videos converter program. Fig.2e shows Animoto website where slideshows can be converted into videos.

DVDs

DVDs are a common way of selling digital products. You can burn your MP4 Video onto a DVD and sell it online on popular eStores such as Amazon, eBay, and others.

There are various ways by which you can have DVD products. Either you can create the DVD yourself or you can take advantage of the various online facilities available to do this for you, at a small fee.

Fig. 2f TrepStar DVD making and publishing

TrepStar is such a nice concept that saves you from the hassles of raising capital to make economic bundles of DVDs and CDS, which range from 200 DVDs/CDs or over at a time. At TrepStar you only need to create content for one CD or DVD, have a logo for the cover page, and upload the content plus the logo. Everything else will be done for you, right from designing the cover to burning on-demand CDs and DVDs, marketing them, selling them, and handling all financial transactions on your behalf. You only need to check your account status and withdraw the rewards of your creativity – All these at only $5 per DVD or CD!TrepStar is the best way to go if you don't want to commit a lot of money for a product you are not sure would pay up for the cost and reward you with handsome profits.

Kunaki is another place to create your DVDs and CDs. The good thing about Kunaki, unlike TrepStar, is that it provides free barcodes. A barcode is mandatory if you would like to sell your products on major eStores such as Amazon. This would save you the cost and time of developing the barcode and make it easy for you to sell your DVDs and CDs on multiple online stores.

Fig. 2g Kunaki online DVD creation and publishing

EBooks

EBooks are fast becoming the best and most loved way to have book presentation. Once you have created your video, you can easily transcribe it into an eBook. You don't need to worry about the effort and time since there are various ghostwriters online whom you can outsource this work to be done on your behalf. Check on 'How to outsource common tasks' in our table of contents for details.

Fig 2h Bookpatch on demand printing and publishing

The good thing is that you don't need to be an expert in creating various forms of eBooks. You need first to create your eBook in MS Word format.

Once your eBook is in Word format, you can convert it to any format needed for an online eBook or printed book!

Fig.2h shows an excerpt from the Book Patch website. BookPatch is an on-demand self-publishing site, whereby you can upload your Word formatted eBook and it is automatically converted into an online eBook format. The advantage of BookPatch is that the book can be sold as an eBook or be printed as hardcopy. Unlike ordinary hardcopy printing, this is on-demand printing where you need not commit huge printing costs incurred as a result of printing in bulky volumes, so as to make economic sense. On-demand printing makes better economic sense, since a single or multiple copies can be printed by the customer as he or she demands.

Other eBook formats include the Kindle format for Amazon, Nooks format for Barnes and Noble, ePub, Mobi, and others. Kindle eBook format is the most popular, and the good thing is that you can easily upload your Word eBook with minor modifications, as per Amazon requirement, to allow it to be converted to Kindle eBook.

Slides

A slideshow is one of the easiest and most attractive ways of presenting your content; be it an eBook, product demo, product description, user instructions manual, events gallery, and many other types of content that you would like to show.

Slideshows have traditionally been confined to desktop publishing, mainly by the use of PowerPoint. However, with business going online, a need for online slideshow presentation became inevitable. SlideShare, as depicted by Fig.2i, shows an online slide presentation.

Figure 2i presentation by SlideShare

Once you have created your PowerPoint presentation, you only need to upload it onto SlideShare, follow basic instructions, and all else will be done automatically.

10 Easy Ways to Finance the Launching of a New Product:

You might have a great idea and you are confident enough that it will be a top seller in the market. Without great ideas, it is impossible to have success. In the same way, having the necessary capital is a vital part of your product development and marketing. Without proper funding, your ideas will not become the ray of hope for your business. The idea will get stuck in the primary stage. To make your ideas fruitful, here are some great tips for you to help you launch your new product.

1. Financing from Family and Friends

If it is a brand new business, financing could come from your family and friends. If this is the case, you should treat your friends and family members seriously like you would other lenders or investors. This means that you should have a proper loan document drawn up between them and yourself, and you should pay them back with interest on the loan.

2. Licensing a Product Idea to a Big Company

Getting a license for a brand company, means that you allow them to sell your product while you take a percentage of the profit. In this case, you should acquire the services of an attorney to draw up an agreement between you and the company so that you can enjoy a fair share of the profit from sales of your product. You have to be careful so that company doesn't sell your idea as their own idea. Deal with everything cautiously, including the patents, the registration and agreement, and you can start your journey with a famous big company.

3. Peer-to-Peer Lending

In this kind of financing, you can take loans from individuals at various lending sites like Prosper.com or LendingTree.com. This kind of alternative lending provides both business and personal loans which often have lower interest rates than old-fashioned bank loans and there is also less paperwork.

4. Crowdfunding

This is almost like peer-to-peer lending, but with some significant differences. Firstly, rather than taking a loan, crowdfunding folks make a donation to your business or idea, generally in return for early access to your product, or a specific version of the product or some other exceptional treatment.

Crowdfunding works best for products which are easy to perceive, exciting and consumer-oriented. For special niche markets, like a video game, socially responsible customers or early technology adopters will be enthusiastic about crowdfunding. You will find popular crowdfunding sites on the Internet, such as Kickstarter and IndieGoGo.

5. Trade or Vendor Credit

In trade or vendor credit, your suppliers give you an extended time to pay them for the materials, which you need to brand your fresh product. If you can get 90-day terms assigned, this may provide the funding you need to launch your new product. In this time, you can sell enough of your products to pay the vendor's loans.

Trade credit works for established businesses launching new products. If you are confident, and have a good business plan, you'll be able to pay your vendor's loans within the specific time.

6. Pre-Sales

If you have an existing business, you may be able to pre-sell your idea before developing your product. The best strategy is to offer your customers a good discount on the product, which will encourage them to buy it. If you think that you have enough pre-sales, you can sell it at the full price to other consumers.

7. Subscription Sales

Subscription sales work well for products that need to be purchased on a regular basis, such as cosmetics, or personal care products, or pet food. By selling annual or quarterly subscriptions, you can make enough income to finance production.

8. Purchase Order Financing

In purchase order financing, a lender advances you money based on your products. You use that money for the production.

9. Business Line of Credit

If you have a successful business with a track record of at least 3 or 4 years, you may be able to get a business line of credit from a bank or financial institute which enables you to draw the credit line up to a maximum amount during the production period.

10. Credit Card Financing

Financing a new product with credit cards is costly. But if you think that you can sell enough of the product to pay off the charges, using credit cards to purchase the materials can work.

How to Get Funding for your Product Development and Marketing

Fig 2j Raising money through Indiegogo

Are you financially hard-hit so that you cannot develop your product? Kickstarter is there to kickstart your idea. Kickstarter is a place where those with viable ideas that they would like to develop into products can get a funding boost. You simply need to publish your idea on Kickstarter explaining its viability and your target fund, not forgetting to highlight, of course, the kind of benefit that would accrue to your funders. Another online place to get funds to finance your idea is Indiegogo. Kickstarter is more favourable for artistic ventures while Indiegogo is for general business ideas or products.

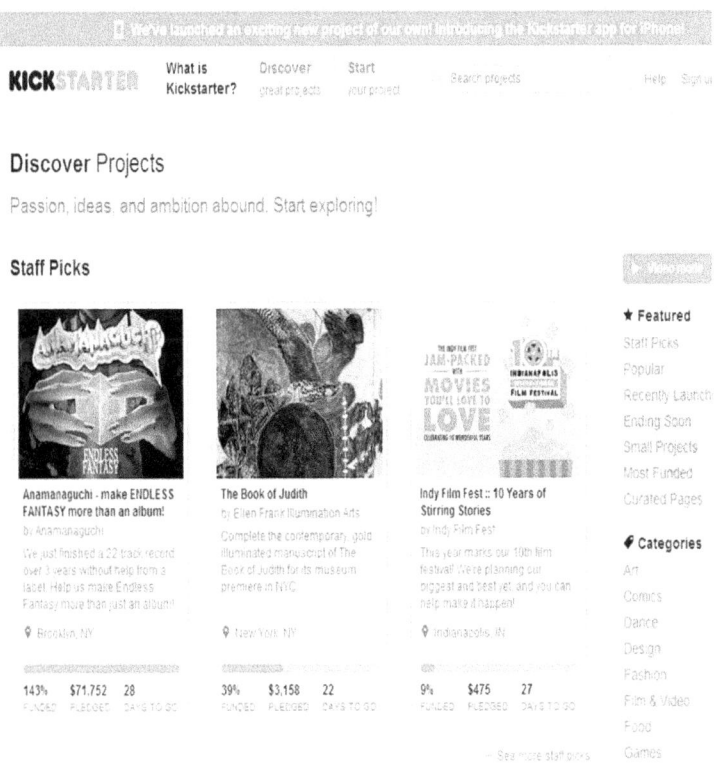

Fig 2k Kickstarter project funding

How to Find a Market for Your Products

Fig. 3 Products must be in the right form to be valuable

The product that you intend to sell must have value to your prospective customers. To have this value, the product must have utility – that is, the ability to satisfy customers' wants. The product must have the utility of time, utility of place, and utility of form. Utility of time simply means that the product must be delivered at the right time. Utility of place means that the product must be delivered at the right place. Utility of form means that the product must be delivered in the right form.

To ensure that your product has value, you must conduct market research. The greatest mistake people make is creating a product thinking that it is such a great product that people will be falling over to buy it. You've got to start with market research first in order to identify customers' wants, so that you can tailor and package your product in such a manner that increases its value to your target customers.

As depicted by fig.4 there are several critical steps that you must follow in ensuring that your product becomes a product of great value to your target customers, especially when you intend to sell your product online.

FINDING A HOT MARKET

- • It contains a large number of people
- • These people are irrationally passionate
- • They have disposable income
- • They have their own jargon
- • They have their own magazines
- • They may hold their own conferences and events
- • They have their own celebrities

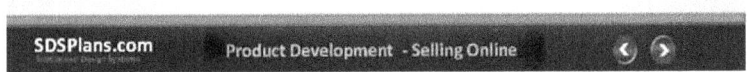

Fig. 4 Finding a Hot Market

Finding a Hot Market

How do you find a hot market? Finding a hot market requires a combination of skills, experience, and intuition. It is not a straight walk in the park. Nonetheless, there are several tips that can guide you on the way to finding that hot market for your product.

ONLINE SUCCESS FORMULA

- Step One - Find a "HOT MARKET"
- Step Two - Ask the market what they want
- Step Three – Develop or find a product and sell it to them
  - – A market is a group of people who share a passionate interest in a particular topic.

SDSPlans.com   Product Development - Selling Online

Fig 5 Online Success

As depicted by fig. 5, the top 7 tips for finding a hot market are;

1. **It contains a large number of people**. The bigger the volume of sales the bigger the profits, therefore, you need to find a market with a large number of people to make those huge profits you are wanting.

2. **These people are irrationally passionate**. Having a market characterized by irrationally passionate people is like discovering a shallow goldmine characterized by almost pure gold deposits. You simply need little effort to get that high value. Highly rational people are hardly passionate and buy things because they need them and not because they want them. On the other hand, highly irrational people are extremely passionate; they do buy things because it appeals to their wants and not necessarily their needs.

3.   **They have disposable income**. To an Accountant, disposable income refers to that income that you are left with after meeting all the tax obligations and other mandatory deductions from your payroll or gross income. However, to a marketer, disposable income is what is freely available after meeting mandatory expenses that are not just tax and other payroll deductions. It excludes deductions such as rent, school fees, utility expenses, and other mandatory living expenses, so that what is left as disposable income is that money that you can actually 'gamble' with. Yes, this is what can irrationally spent! One great mistake that many businesspeople make is to target just a large population without evaluating whether or not the respective population has purchasing power to buy the products. The higher the disposable income, the higher the purchasing power.

4.   **They have their own jargon**. Yes, people of the same class find a common language to express their common values. If your target market comprises of people who have met the first three criteria and yet they do have their own jargon, then, you've struck a goldmine. Communication is the secret code that helps you to influence your customers' psychology. Once you've mastered their jargon, you've discovered the secret code not only to learn their tastes and preferences, but also to re-program their mindset to value and appreciate your products.

5.   **They have their own magazines**. Do you know the role magazines play in marketing? Magazines are not only a source of advertisement space, but also a great way to learn consumers' lifestyles. If a certain magazine is a hit in a certain market, then, it is

a magazine that represents a lifestyle that market has or aspires to have.

6. **They may hold their own conferences and events**. This is another place to learn not only the tastes and preferences of your potential customers, but also the place to learn their lifestyle and behavioral pattern. Attending and participating in such conferences and events is the surest way to learn the secrets of how you need to package your products to suit your potential customers.

7. **They have their own celebrities**. Just like magazines, conferences, and events, celebrities are a pointer to the lifestyle, tastes, and preferences of a particular market segment. Nonetheless, it is also a manifestation of the behavioral patterns of customers within that market segment. By observing celebrities and comparing them with other markets, you would easily understand what interests your potential customers and what turns them off. This would go a long way in helping you package your product in a way that presses that 'passionate irrational button'.

Ask the Market What They Want?

Yes, before you develop a product for a certain target market you need to understand what that particular market is looking for. The challenge is - how do you go about it? There are various ways by which you can inquire and get information of a certain target market and first and foremost, is by reading the market. You can read a particular market by observing its trend, lifestyle, tastes, and preferences from sources such as TVs, Magazines, Newspapers, Blogs, and even social media such as Facebook. Secondly, you can choose to do market survey. Market survey can easily be done online by use of online questionnaires right on your site or social media. Making use of online survey tools such as survey monkey or if you can afford it, engaging a market research company to perform market research on your behalf, is a great idea.

Develop or Find a Product and Sell It to Them

You can choose to either develop a product for your target market or simply find an existing product to sell to the target market.

Some people feel that finding an existing product to sell is not such a great idea. However, great ideas are not the ones that sell or bring success. What brings product success in the market is the execution. Therefore, if you can find an existing product to sell, then devise an appropriate execution strategy that is much better than the existing strategies and you will succeed.

Nonetheless, should you not find a suitable existing product to sell, you would need to develop one. However, you need not necessarily labor so much to re-invent the wheel. Simply make a better wheel. What this means is that it is safer and less risky to redesign and repackage an existing product than to develop a completely new novel idea that you are not sure of how customers would respond to it.

Product-vs-market what comes first? This is a question that is clearly depicted by fig. 6. Yes, it is a chicken-versus-egg kind of question. Whether a product or a market comes first depends so much on your thought – whether you are a producer-oriented or marketer-oriented person. Would you start with a great idea first, or a great market first? It is a great market that shapes a great idea. Thus, before you develop a great product, there has to a great market for it.

Fig 6 Product VS Market

How to Sell Your Products Online

Selling products online is one of those exhilarating experiences. It is fun to do. However, not everyone experiences this fun. To succeed in selling online, you need to heighten your search probe and receptive antenna. Yes, it is an adventure that needs tricky exploratory techniques and probing prowess. You've got to understand how to approach the market! You need not get scared though, it is just one of the easiest adventures to make. Here we simplify it for you.

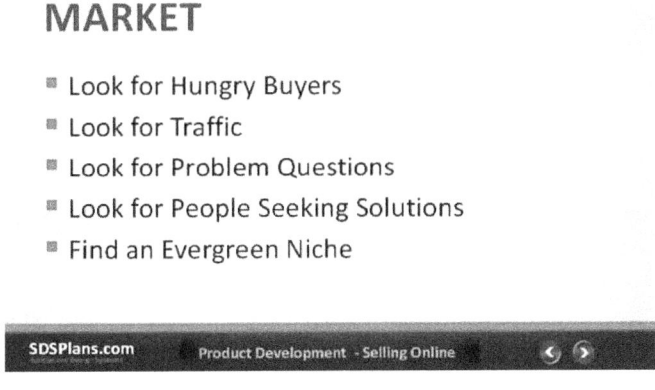

Fig 7 How to approach online market

Fig.7 depicts the top 5 tips on how to approach online market in order to sell your product;

1.   **Look for hungry buyers**. Hungry buyers are those buyers with an insatiable appetite for something else that will satisfy their wants.

These are the people who will rush to buy your satisfying product once you launch it.

2.   **Look for traffic**. Just as you would like to locate your physical shop at a site with a heavy traffic of people, you naturally desire to place your online product on sites with heavy traffic flow of visitors.

3.   **Look for problem questions**. Ask, ask, and ask! You need to find that great problem to solve. The greater the problem, the greater the solution. If you really want your product to be a great product in the market, then, it must be a product that offers a great solution to the great problem in that market.

4.   **Look for people seeking solutions**. Yes, there is one thing to have a problem and it is out rightly a different thing to seek solutions. Not all people who have a problem are seeking solutions to their problem. There are those who have surrendered to the problem and trying to wake them from their self-inflicted surrender is like trying to flog a dead horse. On the other hand, there are those who have a problem that they don't even know that the problem exists! In both cases, you would have to be ready to work harder to convince them that you have a solution. The easiest people to convince are those who know the kind of a problem they have and are actively seeking solutions. These are the people who, once you launch your product, would silently shout 'Eureka!' and would most likely rush in droves to buy your product.

5.   **Find an evergreen niche**. A great farmer knows that the best trees to provide shade to him and his cattle during hot and dry season, and yet still provide cover during rainy season, are those trees that

are evergreen. Yet, this is the same secret that works so well when it comes to marketing. You need not spend lots of your dollars investing in developing a product that will soon perish or become obsolete. You would rather spend your money, time, and effort developing a product that is evergreen, that is, a product with a long life cycle and would still earn you some revenue irrespective of the economic cycles.

Once you've satisfied the above listed criteria or tips, then you are in for proper selling online. The most important thing, before fully launching your product into the market, is you have to do market testing or test marketing so as to gauge the customer's response before channeling all your energies to aggressive marketing. This would help you determine whether the product, as developed, meets customers wants and expectations or whether you would need to repackage it or develop it further or even withdraw it altogether. It is better to withdraw a non-selling product than incur loses trying to force it through the throats of unwilling buyers.

24 Easier Ways to Make First Online Sale

Selling your first product online is very important, and, beginning your sales on the online portal is also a symbolic journey. You will find courage, inspiration and optimism from your first online sale. It will even bring a great turning point for your company and your business life. Remember one thing, you must be careful not to be misled by your first product's sale. It is difficult to get the first customer and is comparable to a battle. You must think that you are in the battle field and conducting a battle with your opponent. To win the battle the following catchy ideas will help you prepare for the first online sale.

1. Send Samples to the people who have influence on others

In the world of the internet, there are so many efficient bloggers, entrepreneurs, journalists, and bloggers from various niches and industries. Many of these companies have large audience and followers on their websites and social media sites.

Sending free gifts will provide you with the opportunity to meet with the influencers who are directly or indirectly related to your industry. In this way you will get the opportunity to introduce yourself to them and you can appreciate and like their work. In this way they will be encouraged to mention you ion their online website or on the platform they use which will be helpful for your company and for your start-up.

By introducing yourself to them you will not only get the traffic, but you will also get the seal of approval from the industries and experts. In this way you will be able to attract the customer to your products. Customers will even be able to judge the products in comparison to the products of other companies. The best result you can achieve from the influencers is that they will provide you with measureable results to follow up on potential leads.

2. Blogging can give you a turn

You should start blogging as soon as possible. If you are not doing your blogging that means you are missing limitless potential from content marketing. It is the most influential way to reach the customer and you can easily inform your customers by using keywords techniques. You must provide useful and appropriate content to attract customers and to inform them about the quality of the products. In this way you will get the search engine ranking and will get the best chance to influence social media.

Now you need to think about the topic and content of the blog. The simplest way to highlight your product is to provide product related information in your blog content. With new products people have many questions. You can write your blog and use it to address those questions and related problems and issues. It is normal that people will ask about your company and products and the product's benefit. So, you can simply write your blog on this topic initially. Remember your initial blog should be catchy and motivate people's interest in your product.

For instance, Shopify visitors are interested in knowing about e-commerce. For this reason, Shopify has created a content blog with how to shop and how online selling works. In the same way, you can write about your product and its use in everyday life so that by searching people can find your product easily.

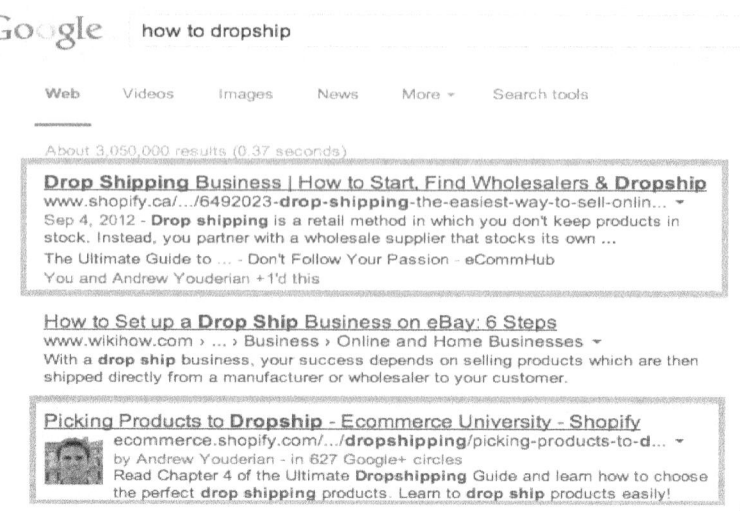

4

Along with this, you can provide some tips and techniques related to the products and some resources for their use. You can even give some ideas and lifestyle tips from people related to your products. You will understand content marketing, if you begin to create content on a regular basis. You will find ways to promote your product everywhere, using social media, search engine optimization and so forth.

3.   Email List Building

It is crucial to create an email list for your marketing. According to the research of MarketingSherpa, 60% to marketers found that email marketing generates return on investment ROI (BEFORE YOU USE THIS acronym YOU must first cite the full term) or the company and 32% believe that it will ultimately generate ROI. The research found that 119% ROI is generated from email marketing. So, it is impossible to ignore this area of marketing.

The main advantage you get from an email list is that you send your product information into their inbox. By comparison, due to time zone differences and user preferences, using social media like Facebook, twitter, etc. you may not send your product's information so successfully. By having and using the email list, you can treat them as your regular personal clients.

How can you build your email list? You can start an email subscription on your website where most of the visitors will notice it. It is a little tricky to convince e customers to sign up for your product's list. It has been found that the visitor to your site never signs up for free. To motivate the customers, you need to send some offers or incentives. For example, Skinny Teatox offers a competition to win a product free every week. In this way they encourage people to join their subscription list.

About

Skinny Teatox is the #1 teatox in the United States and Canada.

Made with 100% natural ingredients that promote good health and weight loss.

Enter to Win a Free 14 Day Teatox!

Enter our free contest to win a 14 Day Teatox.

your@email.com   Sign Up

4. Sponsoring a relevant event

For some particular products, sponsoring a relevant event works. But some people think that it could be wasting resources and time. So, to find out the appropriate event, you need to do your research.

Firstly, you must ensure that you have selected the right sponsor or event. Just think about the event in which your customer will be interested and then decide how many clients will be present at that event.

After making rough ideas about the event size and type, you can think about the cost of the event. It is not enough to just set up tables and hand out flyers. Rather, if you think that the event has potential you should be more creative and use it to build a better relationship with the customers.

At the event you should present the most attractive products to inform the people about your start-up. To attract more customers, you can, for example provide some free samples which act as rewards and coupons, which, along with free stickers will enable you to get the personal contact and emails and opportunity to follow up using social media.

5. Interview with industry influencers

Interviewing industry influencers is considered one of the best ways to sell your first product online. Interviews work as a win win situation. The interviewee gets publicity through which he can be famous and you can get some valuable content from the interviewee to publish on your website and share it on social media alongside your blog.

You must be careful that the questions you ask are relevant and related to your products. So, you will not only ask them about their lives and career, but also you will ask about his business and industry. From the interview some people will respond to their personality and some people will get advice from their business experience. For example, interviewing Elena Shumilova, popular in the world of photography, provided great content for web-based photo vendors.

6. Pulling a PR stunt

Pulling a PR stunt can be the trick if you want the fast sales. It works like a viral video that is made based on the same concept which works to promote your brand. In this process, you will get instant publicity and so, you will gain some loyal customers. Actually, a PR Stunt is something which does something unusual and, often, hilarious to attract media attention. If it can be done properly, your store will get lots of links from the news source and its authority which will quickly bring an increase traffic, and will be helpful for search engine optimization (SEO)

In this case, Virgin is an example of the best type of PR Stunt. Founder Richard Branson dressed as a bride and jumped out from a casino, acting like a Zulu warrior. He also drove a tank over coke cans on Fifth Avenue in New York, and flew a balloon across the world.

7. Try AdWords

AdWords is the most popular Google advertisement network that helps people to advertise on Google search results, like YouTube or partner websites. You can easily rank in the top three in the search. For example, when searching Samsung TV you will find the following in the Google search engine.

The best thing about AdWords is it has a capacity for massive reach. Within a few minutes, you can set up your advertising campaign with your text and image or videos and it will be seen by visitors all over the web. Through AdWords, you can make target ads which are displayed beside Google searches. In addition to this, your ads also will appear on every website containing similar keywords.

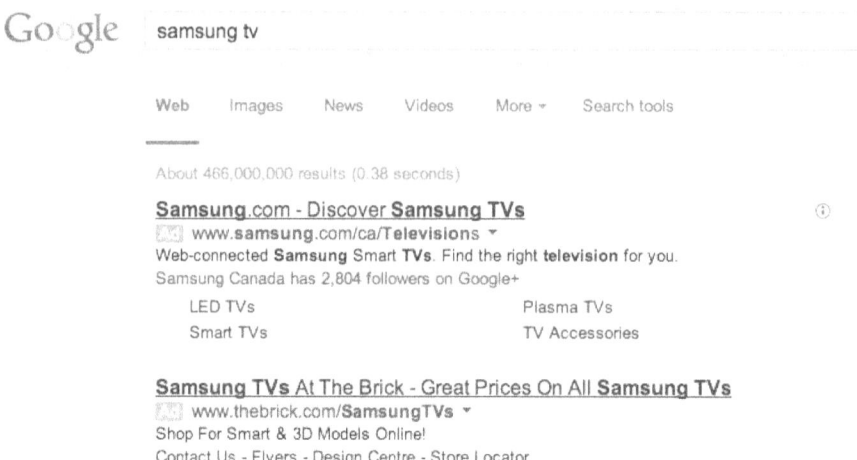

8. Sharing your traffic with affiliated markets

It is difficult to sell your product alone. So share the load with others. Affiliate Marketing will help you market your products and bring huge traffic to your website. In this case you may offer the affiliates a percentage. For your affiliate marketer you can provide ID and a code to set up the links in their own personal websites or blog.

For instance, if a website owner posts your link for a Watch for sale and some visitor buys that product when visiting his website, you will give a percentage to the website owner. The affiliate marketing schemes depend on two things, i.e. the types of products and the commission you provide to your partner.

9. Selling wholesale to retailers

You will obviously sell your products to the customers, but there is nothing wrong in selling your products to wholesalers. The main advantage of wholesale is it increases cash flow into your business. You may get less profit but you are shifting your products in bigger quantities. Along with this, through this, you are involving other companies in marketing your products to customers. It will help your publicity and thus boost your sales!

10. Publishing press releases

In order to attract media attention, many new online stores send out press releases. But most of the time they cannot attract customers because of the poor quality of the press release. Instead of attracting customers it demoralizes them. Your Press Release must be professional, catchy, and short. Remember that the people like something interesting. People always avoid monotonous things.

11. Paying attention to analysis and statistics

Website analytics and review is important so you can understand the behavior of customers and web visitors. You can easily understand why you are getting profit or why you cannot. From the analytics you will understand what your customers are doing, the pages they have visited and the time they spent on your website and the source from which they have come to visit your site. There are some tools through which you can get additional information on how frequently customers browse your site.

You might think about the cost. Never think about that. You need not spend a penny - it is completely free. In Miracle Berry you will find an example where you can see the steady traffic. They have got this traffic either through social media or paid placement.

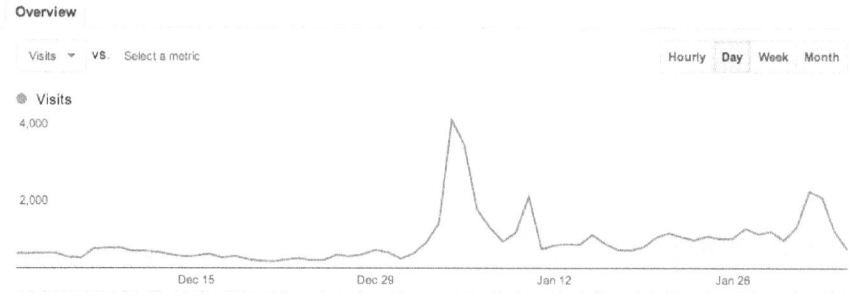

After launching your online store, you fight for your sales. It is undoubtedly important to analyze your visitors. You never know what you are going to learn from this traffic analysis.

12. Running a survey

If you can understand the motive and the desire of the customers, you can easily adapt your business and can go forward. Surveys are considered as a source of honest feedback. Like your family members they will provide you with an authentic review either of your products' quality and/or price. You will find many online surveys like Survey Monkey and Qualaroo for creating online surveys.

13. Network on the forums

The Online discussion forum is a great place to share tips, advice, question answer, customer quires, etc. related to business.

In this case you can find out some active forums in the Google or Yahoo search that might be related to your products. When you post in the forum, you must be careful that you are not violating any rules and regulations of the products. You must know the restrictions and the limit of the products and of course you have to obey them accurately. The rules include signature, avatar, profile page.

You may desire to promote widely, but you have to control your desire and emotion, maintaining your professionalism in the forum. It is absolutely undesirable if you post in the forum always with the link to your website. If you do such activities, you will damage your online brand to the other forum members. So, instead of spam post, you should post quality content so that people can appreciate your content and know about your brand. In the net world you will find two popular forum, i.e. Digital Point and Warrior Forum, which have been working with helpful communities.

14. Set up a Cartel

Sometimes, it's better to get the support from the outside. So taking a small online cartel may be the best trick. Find a retailer to support each other. In this way you can gain various ways of selling. To explain, if you run an online clothing shop, your perfect cartel may be the footwear outlets and jewelry. Your partner shop will be almost similar but there will have no conflict of interest. You should think about the private setup in order to attract more members to build a supportive community. Like e-commerce Group via Facebook. They have more than 2500 members who always share e-commerce ideas, give advice and now and then provide help.

15. Build the right relationships

In the online business it is who you know it is not what you know. You should build relationship, both online and offline. In this way you can get success. It does not matter what kind of product you sell. You should always remember that you had better friend with the like-minded person. Remember that you should not collaborate with your competitors. For instance, you should collaborate with websites, bloggers ad suppliers who actually focus on your industry and they will also provide you consumer feedback and offer promotional deal.

16. Offer a contest

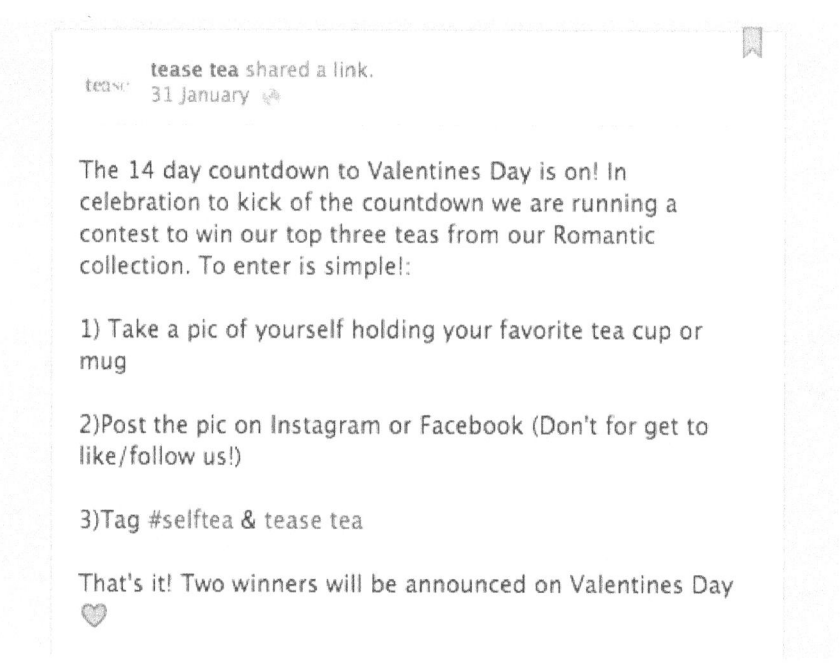

Most of the consumers love free gift. On the other hand, launching the competition, you can build the trust among the consumers. In this way, you will get the link with people and some other organizations. It will not only build relationships, but also it will build trust among the people. You need not launch a big event. Recently, Tease Tea, a new online tea store has run so simple contest on their Facebook page.

For this type of contest, you need not spend any money just you need to spend a few minutes! There are some online service providers like ViralSweep and Gleam who will help you   to launch a contest with simple and professional way without adding extra work.

17. Begin Tweeting

With simple ways in twitter you can engage with your target market. It is the best way to find potential customers who actually ask some questions regarding products and your industries. You can easily reach out them by twitter.

The aim of your twitter is not to mention your products rather your twitter will be helpful for the customers. For example, when Gary Vaynerchuk was twitting about Wine Library, he offered advice; he did not pitch.

So people will be grateful and will be eager to know about him and ultimately discover his business. This might work for your first online sale.

For a real life example, you can read some tweets from the online jewelry store Lola Rose.

18. Engage on LinkedIn

In the Linkedin, you will find all types of professional and executives connected with each other. After launching your e-commerce business, you can get connected with some executives or members of another company. You may sell your product directly to them, but you will discover huge opportunities with other companies, websites' owners or suppliers. Among the vast public and private companies you can post your questions and converse with others regarding your products.

19. Engage with Pinterest, Instagram, and Vine

If you want to represent your creativity and personality, you can take the best help from their big social media like Pinterest, Instagram, and most recently Vine which are regarded as the best platform for online sale. With slightly different ways you can engage with your customers in these platforms.

Just take pics and videos of your products, even you can show the production process of your products. You can tell your story with videos and images. You should always aim for beauty as people love beauty. For instance, you can have a look at the new online cosmetic store Melt Cosmetics who has already over 150,000 followers on Instagram.

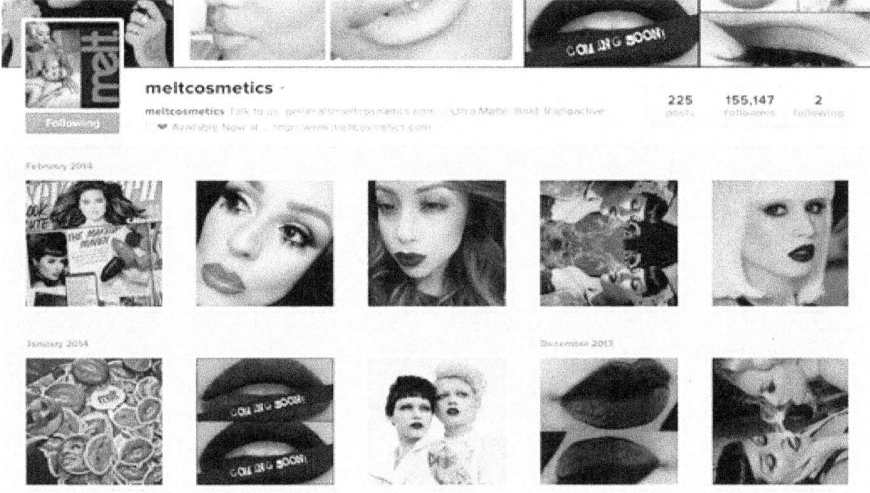

With beautiful photograph they are building a brand image.

20. Never forget Facebook

Never ever, avoid Facebook as it is still considered as the social media powerhouse. Engage with your personal Facebook profile and your business page and let the people know about your company and your products. With creative updates, interact with group and talk about your products in the fun page.

You should remember the Facebook ad in mind like Adwords by which you can create targeted campaigns to get more like and thus you can promote your sale and brand. For instance, a popular drying salon in Toronto named Drybar has huge engagement with Facebook community of over 80,000 who always share ideas related to drying.

21. Beat the competition on shopping engines

Many visitors roam around before final purchase. Even they search in the search engine before purchase. In the popular engines like Google, The find, Shopping and Nextag all of these with huge products are simultaneously compared with the customers. For example, if your search products price in the Find on your favorite hot sauce you will find the following.

You should stay competitive in terms of price. You can take help from the PC Pro who provides a detailed guide on how to get noticed on the Google of Shopping and in the Shopify, you will get 10 most popular comparison shopping engine with little explanation.

22. Make an Infographic

An infographic is the name of the graph of information or visual representation of the statistics that is easy to understand.

UnBounce, which has built an inspiring and detailed guide to marketing with infographics. You won't believe that how popular it is! In the last two years the search with Google has increased 800%. You might be worried whether you will be able to make infographics. Don't worry, there are plenty of firms like Column Five Media provide infographic creative services, focusing on your content.

23. Design your store attractive ways

It is said that first impressions are the best impression and it makes everything. When it comes to selling online, first impressions heavily depends on the best web design. Your website must be user friendly so that visitors can find your brand products without much scrolling. Along with this, navigation through your catalog must be enjoyable and easier. In addition to this, you should build a mobile responsive store. In the age of smart phone it is vital as most of the visitors will visit your store through mobile devices. Recently, it has been found that 55% people do their shopping via mobile phone in comparison to the mobile shopping in 2013 when it was only 45%. So you must emphasis on mobile devices.

24. Hold a Pop-up store

It does not mean that your online store always will be online. Through pop-up store, you can complement your online presence. Don't think about the financial burden of this kind of products as you know that it is temporary.

Before opening a pop up store, you must consider the location. You can either open it at art fairs, farmers markets, galleries and shopping mall, including any other place like people gathering. Make sure that you will get your target market there and that area will be clearly visible.

This store can work as a great offline marketing post. You may distribute your coupon or any price cod to purchase via online from your shop. From here you can collect email and contact details from the customers along with social media info.

How to Conduct Market Testing

Have you ever thought of food that you've never eaten before? Would you order large quantities of it? Definitely not! You would most likely just take one or a few bites of it to have a taste before taking more bites and ordering bigger quantities. The same happens to your new product in the market. You wouldn't expect customers to just buy it in huge quantities straight away. Only those daring enough would buy straight away. Those who are not risk takers would wait to hear what others have experienced before making their bets.

MARKET TESTING

- KSL Ebay Etsy Usfreeads Craigslist
- Kickstarter Indiegogo
- Is There Competition
- Are there Affiliate Options Clickbank
- Local Promotion
- Online Searches, Forums, User Groups

Fig 8 Market Testing

Similarly, a market is just like a new kind of food for you. Just as your customers want a taste bite, so would you want to experience that taste bite of the market before going full blown into releasing more products into it.

Fig.8 depicts some of the places where you can start off. These places include KSL, Ebay, Amazon, Etsy, Craiglist, etc.

KSL.com, ebay.com, and craiglist.com are great places to test market whatever you want to sell online. These places have huge traffic flows and therefore your product has the advantage of exposure.

There are other specialized markets online such as etsy, Kunaki, and trepstar. Etsy is suitable for selling artistic homemade handicrafts.

Selling Digital Products

In case you would like to sell digital products such as books, movies, and music, then you do have an upper hand for many more places. Places such as Kunaki and trepstar are ideal for digital products such as DVDs. Indeed, if you are a starter and you don't have much capital, trepstar is such a wonderful place for you. You just need to create a small logo for your DVD and trepster will create an impressive cover, burn the DVDs, sell them, and handle financial transactions on your behalf at only $5 per piece sold. Kunaki also does the same and provides a bar code for your DVDs. Bar codes are a must in case you would like to sell your products on Amazon.

If you are dealing with eBooks, there are several places for you, including Amazon and Bookpatch. Bookpatch has an extra advantage over Amazon – simplicity. At Bookpatch, you only need to upload your eBook in word document format and everything else will be taken care of. Also, at Bookpatch, your eBook gets listed immediately. The other advantage of

Bookpatch over Amazon is that Bookpatch offers on-demand printing for hard copies, while Amazon would require you to avail already printed books as hard copies. Amazon does have a new service called Createspace that will allow you to develop on demand printed books and offers them to the Amazon market and other bookstores.

Selling through Affiliates

Is your product such that you do need mass marketing yet you can't afford to employ and manage a huge army of salespeople? Selling through affiliates is the right model for you. Yes, there are online sites that provide a huge Salesforce that is affiliated to them and are ready and willing to sell products on your behalf placed on those sites.

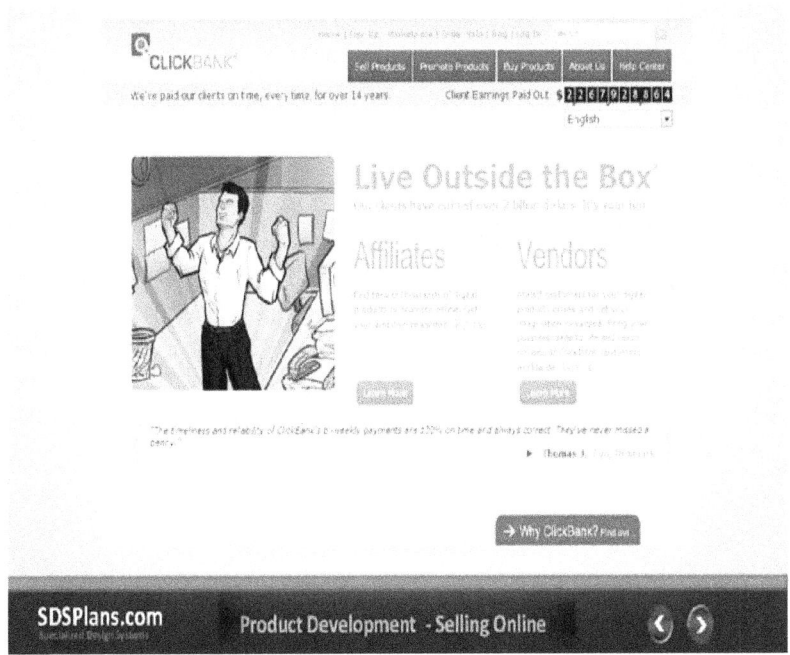

Fig 9 Clickbank affiliate marketing

Such a famous site is Clickbank. Clickbank is such a place to do test marketing since it has thousands of affiliates who will market your products on their sites. This would expose your products to thousands of sites on the internet within an extremely short time. Imagine launching your product and within hours, it is being displayed on thousands of sites! This can't be possible on the normal brick-and-mortar model of selling.

Other than Clickbank, there are various other affiliate sites online, such as SFI, which operates in a similar fashion, although SFI is more of a multi-level marketing model.

How to predict if a Product or Service will Sell before Launching:

Certainly, you are excited with your new products or service, but how can you know that your new products or service will be bought by the customers. You need not spend huge amounts of money to test the market. By following some strategies you can test your product's market and can figure out before launching your product, whether there is a market of your products. It will work like magic for your products if you can apply it in the proper place and time.

Begin With Friends and Family

It has been found that the majority of the market research begins with getting feedback from your friends and family. You can converse with your family over a meal in the car to inform them about your creation. Simply, you just want to know whether your ideas are worthy. Do the people need this product? Will they spend money for this product? The people in your life will be more positive about your new products. So, if you don't find positive answers from your dearest one, you must think that there is a problem.

For example, you want to launch a product for the younger generation like a tool by which they can easily organizer their day to day activities. At first give it to your family members and tell them to use it. The members of your family will definitely tell about the pros and cons of the products as they are well-wisher for your products and for you. They will never hide anything about your products rather they will spontaneously tell you the truth. From their honest review you can certainly understand what should you do to rectify your products and service. Then in the second time, you can again get the review from your dearest and nearest one. After that if you think that your product is ok, you can go for the launch.

Small Scale Testing

After this stage if you want to move forward, you need to test your product in the small scale. If your product is physical, get the feedback on its design and its functions. On the other hand, if you want to sell your service, online business or mobile app, find out the overall satisfaction of the products. Never avoid people's criticism and take all feedback to reshape your products. Remember that if so many people find problems with your product that means you have a problem with your product and you should solve it as soon as possible.

At this stage, you will get an opinion from the people with whom you have no personal relationship. To perform the test on a wider scale you can get the help of the social media and you can appoint some volunteers who will work for you in the social media. After getting the data you can take the decision whether you will launch your product public at large.

Testing the Market Online

The Internet is the biggest platform to test your product and you can do your test in a different ways. You can do it by online forum observing the frequency of the post and the numbers the members of the forum. These metric will tell you the activity of the forum and you will get the idea how many people are interested in your products.

In addition to this, Google Insights, Google Trends and the Google Keyword Planner will help you to understand people's searching terms, location of the customers. You cannot predict from this service, whether your business will be successful, but you can use this data to reshape your business. To find the more specialized data you can take help from the sites Quantcast and Market Samurai which will work for you as invaluable resources.

Quantcast will provide you the demographic breakdown of your prospective clients. If there are any websites similar to your one, Quantcast will bring huge information about that site, including gender, age and income level. This information will help you to launch your ideas and advertise your products. On the other hand, Market Samurai will inform you about the number of customers who look for the products and service which you offer.

Don't Fear Competition

When you will come up with your brilliant ideas for your products, you will find that there are many similar products and service are in the market. Don't be disheartened. Have patience, you are most probably going to encounter competition. You will be astonished to hear that every single day the iTunes App Store receives over 1,000 new app submissions.

Instead of being disheartened you should be encouraged as there are huge demand of this product in the market, that's why there are a number of companies who have come to launch their products. In addition to this, a crowd market place always helps you to become more creative and work heart and soul to make your position secure.

In order to get success you just need to differentiate your service or products, branding it in a new way presenting it at the best way possible among the crowd.

All these market research may not be exciting. However, testing the market is an essential part of the business to get success.

Get the Online and Social Media Reviews

You can get the honest opinion of the social media users. Before going to launch, give the use and description of your products. Describe what kind of benefit they can get from your products. Make a video of your products and put it on the YouTube. Just let the people know about your product. Publish a picture and photo of your product or service. From the social media you can understand the people's opinion, their liking and disliking.

As online is a bigger platform, from the social media you can easily get the opinion of the mass people. This opinion will provide you the opportunity to upgrade your products. Even you will understand that whether people want to have your products. You will easily understand the curiosity and demand of the products. Just read the comment of the common people from the social media like Facebook, Twitter, Instagram, Tumber and LinkedIn.

At the same time, you can get two kinds of benefit from the social media site, i.e. one is you are informing people that you are coming to market and at the same time you are getting the view about the products whether they need this product. So, before going to launch your products online, just make a video and share it through Facebook, Twitter and YouTube along with other social media.

Take a Good Preparation:

There is a saying that well begin is half done. While you are going to launch your products, keep all people and things beside you. Always give priority of your time. There are some products which become demandable in the market for the specific time. If you cannot launch the product in that particular time, you cannot reach to your goal.

Before going to launch you need many things like social media publicity, your well-wisher, a team with you who will be with your dream. Even before going to launch, think what you should do for your products. Know the particular culture and lifestyle. In this global age the culture is influencing the people. So, before selecting your products, just know the culture and people's mindset.

Make your money arranged as you know that sometimes you need a good amount of money for your launching. Without thinking anything if you launch your products you cannot go ahead. Even before launching, think about the negative sides of your products. You must think that what will you do if your products get negative impact from the market. Keep people busy. Make ad ready to face that challenge. If you find anything faulty, just sort it out and solve that instantly. If you cannot solve it, your products will be ruined in the bud!

Before going to launch. Check and recheck again and again. After launching anything, it is difficult to rectify that product. If you can take these preparations before launching your products online, it is hoped that you might be the successful businessman on the online market and very soon you will be familiar with all.

Take Consultation from Some Advisers

Of course in the market, you will find someone who knows better than you regarding online business. In the initial stage take some ideas from that experienced person, who will help you to overcome some critical moment. In the online market there is no alternative of experience. But that does not mean that the inexperienced person cannot do online business. Talk with some people who are running business in online. In this case definitely you should talk with such persons who are promoting different types of online business. If you want to take advice from the similar types of different business person. You must be careful. Most of the time you cannot expect honest advice from them as they will consider you their rivals.

So, you had better take suggestions from someone who is promoting different types of business in online. Even, you will be more beneficial if it becomes co-operative business. For example, if you sell clothes online, you should make your business partner or take advice from the jewelry business person. He will certainly provide you honest business advice as he will think that after buying your clothes, he will certainly buy something from the ornament shops. He will never give you negative advice rather he will unconsciously want to make friendship with you and somehow he will tell you to make link with your business so that your customer become diverted to that shops.

It will be one kind of exchange program. When he will help you to make your business bigger, certainly you will feel gratitude and in return you will send your customer to his shop. This give and take policy certainly will help you to launch your product online without any difficulty.

How to Develop Your Product's Website

Fig 10 Website components

Your products website is the most important website when it comes to selling your products. As shown in Fig.10, your page should comprise of 5 critical components; squeeze page, sales page, blog, store, Facebook, and YouTube.

A squeeze page is a page as depicted in Fig.11 that serves the purpose of gathering contact details from visitors to your site. These important contact details includes you visitor's name and your visitor's email address.

A squeeze page allows you to generate an email contact list. An email contact list becomes important when you want to do email marketing.

Through email marketing, you can easily promote your products, take customer surveys, and give special offers to target customers.

Fig 11 Squeeze Page

A sales page is a page where your products are laid out for sale with links to the store. In this page, every product is displayed together with its price. A customer can click on the shopping button displayed as 'Add to shopping cart' in order to add the product to the list of products to purchase. From the shopping cart, there is the 'Check Out' button which a customer clicks after adding all items being bought, so that payments can be made. On the checkout form there are specific details relating to the payment method, e.g. PayPal, Debit/Credit card, etc. Once these details are filled, the customer then clicks on the 'Pay' button to complete the purchase transaction.

A store is basically an extension of the sales page. Once customers click on the 'Buy' or 'Add to shopping cart', they are led to the store where the products can be purchased for download or shipping.

A blog page is a page where extra information is provided that wouldn't otherwise fit in other pages. The blog provides a forum for interaction amongst members and visitors to your site. It also provides an avenue where news about product launches, company policies, product promotions, and other relevant information is found.

Facebook is the most popular social media site. Facebook allows people from all walks of life to interact freely and exchange ideas. With over 1 billion people on Facebook, your website can get huge exposure if you work well on promoting your site on it.

YouTube is one of the top 10 visited sites on the internet today. You can use YouTube to upload video clips that show your product features, demos, and descriptions. You can also use YouTube to showcase your product launch, groundbreaking ideas, and many other important videos.

Techniques on Building a Successful Website for your Business

Before developing a commercial website, you must follow some general guidelines. To get success you need a website which has a professional look, easy navigation, quality content and the best search engine result. If you can implement these necessary elements in your website, you will surely get success in your business.

1. Meet the Customers Need

Think about the scope of your website and make a plan to meet the need of the potential clients. To accommodate expected traffic you need to obtain the correct amount bandwidth. If you want to sell products, be sure that you have a product page which is easier to navigate. In addition to this, you should have contact information by which the customer can easily contact with you. Provide product details along with pictures.

2 Try to Focus on the Professional Look

People take website more seriously, which is designed with professional look along with clean design. Content of your website will be useless, unless you make your navigation easier. Bright colors and high contrast with so many videos and pictures might reduce website's focus. In addition to this, poor quality photos and unorganized data and broken design may present your website like the amateurish.

3. Produce Quality Content

From your quality content the genuine customer will learn about your product. If you can show them that you are helping them by producing quality products, they will definitely trust you. Content is the most powerful things by which you can provide a detailed description of your products. In this way from your content the customers will learn about you and your company. One thing you have to remember that you must write SEO articles so that the customer can find you through their search. And thus after knowing about your product they will feel comfortable buying your products. Develop your product information in such a way so that it becomes easier to understand and become informative.

4. Try to make it Easy to Navigate

Visitors always like easy navigation so that they can find out the information with less clicks. Put your navigation menu in the most visible place so that the visitor can understand the whole concept of the product just by 5 second. If a customer cannot find their products from your website what they need within 30 second it is most probable that they will leave your website and they will visit the competitor's website. To catch your customers and build your brand, you must build a website in which navigation will be clear and easy to follow.

5. Easy Product Purchasing Systems:

Always ensure easy shopping system on your website. You should display your product with some easy description. So while a browsing customer can know about the products and can buy with confidence. Even the selection process must be easier. After selection sometimes customers may change their mind. In that case you need to imply an easier deselect process. Impose a simple, easy shopping cart system. Put various types of payment systems including debit or credit card and online system. Various system will attract customers for the simple purchase.

6. Implement Search Engine Optimization

In this competitive age, you must make your website SEO quality, so that search engine can present the customers quire. Definitely, you want to display your website on the first page of the search engine. That's why you should put such searchable keywords in your website. You should select the key words related to your products. So, when the customer will search, at that time with key words the products will appear in on the page. You should also create Meta and ALT tags to display your website favorably.

7. Keep Your Website Updated

Without updating your website you cannot attract customers as old content or less attractive info cannot attract the customers. So, always try to update your website content. If you update your website on the regular basis, you will find both your old and new customers. Old customers will be happy to get new information and the new customers will get the new product info and they will compare it with other website. When they will trust you that you are an authentic business man, they will trust you and become your long term customers.

How to Generate Traffic to Your Products Website

This page must not only be searchable, but must also provide ease of navigation and valued content to the visitors.

Keyword Research

Where is the traffic & do we focus our efforts
- What keywords get the most traffic
- Competitive analysis
- Buyer keywords vs. DIY keywords
- What would you type in the search box if you were looking to buy your product?

SDSPlans.com   Product Development - Selling Online

Fig 12 Keyword Research

To make your site searchable, you must use SEO (Search Engine Optimization) techniques. Some of these techniques involve:

1. Determining the most important keywords
2. Having an appropriate URL that is rich in Keywords
3. Ensuring that your content is rich in these keywords

4.	Designing your website so that it's coding and navigation is SEO friendly.

Key words are those special words that searchers use to find a certain item online. For example, if someone is interested in learning how to develop online products, most likely the person would type on the search bar 'developing products online'

On the other hand, those who have already developed these products and are seeking ways to sell them online would most likely type on the search bar 'selling products online'. To have the benefit of both worlds, you would combine the two to have 'developing products and selling them online'. This combined keyword is known as a long tail keyword since it is a keyword that comprises other keywords in it and certainly makes up a most likely description of what a searcher would be looking for. The keywords within this long tail keyword are 'developing products' and 'selling online'.

How do you find appropriate keywords that most people use to search online? Most search engines, especially Google, have keyword tools that enable you.

Google Keyword tool, as shown in Fig.13, ranks keywords according to the number of searches per month. The higher the number of searches the more likely your site would be reached if you do use the keyword.

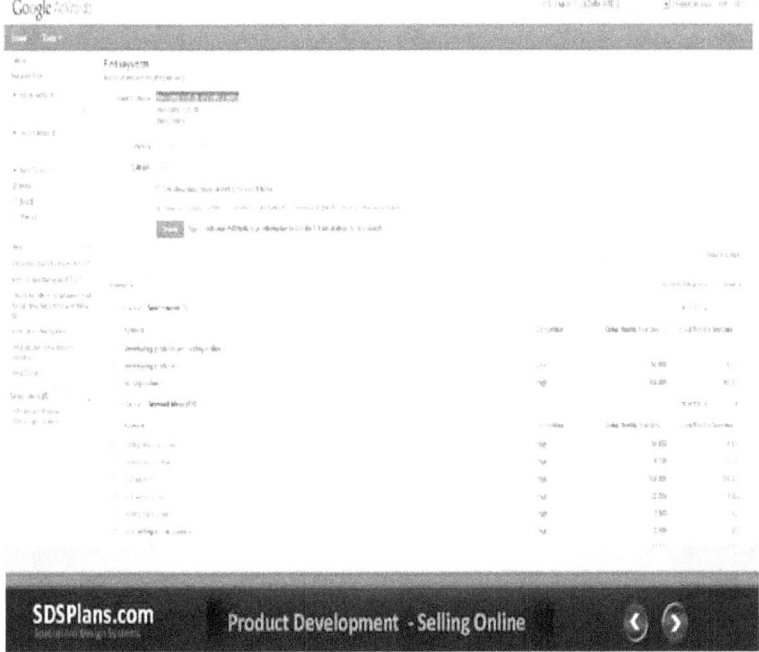

Figure 13 Google Adwords

One important secret is to use longtail keywords as part of your product website's URL. This will not only improve your sites search ability, but also boosts its ranking.

47 Easy Ways to Drive Traffic to Your Website:

More and more web traffic is considered as the best thing for the website and for your business. That's why most of the marketing policy revolves around the attracting traffic to their website. But it is sometimes challenging to bring more traffic to the websites. By following these 49 strategies, you can bring more traffic to your website.

1. Display ads.

Displaying ads on the different websites you can bring more traffic to your websites. In this case you can get a banner or other clickable ads on other sites. Always look for high-traffic sites OutBrain and Taboola are popular who can help you in this case.

2. Try Paid Search Ads.

You can choose Google AdWords and Bing Ads which work as the best. You can chose PPC (pay per click) ad. Based on your key words you can drive traffic to your website.

3. Try social media ads.

Social media like Facebook, Twitter, LinkedIn, YouTube, Instagram, Raddit, etc. will help you to bring traffic to your website. In this modern day social media ads work as best since most of the people always engage with the social media.

4. Attach Your Website to Your Social Media Profiles

Always complete your social media websites as after visiting your social media link the visitors will click into your profile, where they will find your website and click on it.

5. Publish Your Content on Your Social Media

Put your site content in your social media profile where people will find it after visiting a particular social media. If your website is made with WordPress it is better to use Social Warfare plugin to share content easily.

6. Offer Contests on Social Media

To draw more attention to your brand, use social media to host contests. In this way you will find some people who will come to visit your website.

7. Use Calls-to-Action (CTAs) in Social Media Posts

After publishing your content in the social media give people reasons to click on it.

8. Post in Groups in Social Media

Engage with the social media group in LinkedIn, Facebook & Twitter. In this group you will find your identity and publicity which will increase your traffic. In the twitter you can bring more traffic by using hashtags.

9. Repurposing Content

You can use your same content in the different ways. For example, if you have content in the MS word format, you can make it PDF, or it can be made live webinar. Even you can discuss it in the podcast or converting it in the video. As you know different users like different ways to enjoy the contents.

10. Offer Discounts via Social Media or Email

Special offers and discount on your products will bring traffic to your website. You have to give reasons to visit your website to the visitors.

11. Optimize Your Headlines

A recent study has found that 59 shared links in the social media are not clicked at all. So the majority of the articles is not read on the social media. One thing can be easily understood that headlines play a significant role in this aspect. Try to write catchy headlines making it shorter and easier to understand.

12. Optimize Your Site for Search

Take effective SEO strategies with proper Meta tag data, proper coding and structuring.

13. Improve Site's Performance

Ensure that your content loads nice way in all devices like mobile, laptop and desktop and optimize the speed as much as you can.

14. Put better keywords.

Put highly demandable key words in your content. In this way you will go ahead in the search engine competition. The keywords will make your web page higher and bring qualified visitors.

15. Build a Community

It is better to create a forum for your customer to discuss different things related to your brand. The people will come to forum again and again to discuss many things. Though it is time consuming to build such forum but you should invest time to build such forum.

16. Participate in Relevant Industry Forums

It is better to be the part of other industry forum rather than creating an own forum. From the Google search you can find the industry forum

17. Engage with a Blogging Community

You can engage with communities like Problogger or Copyblogger to bring more traffic to your website.

18. Engage with a Slack community.

Slack is a big chat room. In this chat room you will find professional of like-minded industry in your target market. You can consider this community. Here's a list of some Slack communities.

19. Offer Guest Post on Your Blog.

Guest post will help to be acquainted with others. Even they will share the link with your blog and thus you will get the visitors from their website.

20. Build Inbound Links

Build link to other website and that link will help you with SEO and bring more traffic to your website as referral.

21. Remove Bad Links

Using some service like Majestic Ahrefs or Open Site Explorer to eliminate bad links. These bad links will make your search rankings down.

22. Guest Post on Industry Blogs

Become a guest contributor to the industry blog. By this way you will be, familiar with others. For example, you can post your blog here. *The Ultimate, Step-by-Step Guide to Building Your Business by Guest Blogging.*

23. Be Regular Contributor

The person who can contribute regularly can build his brand with a publication audience more quickly than a person who just one post like a guest.

24. Promote Viral Content

Viral contents are still regarded as the best source of web traffic. Create surprising, entertaining or informative content to attract the customers through social media.

25. Put Images in Your Content

It is said that one image is better than one thousand words. Visual contents are more attractive than textual content.

26. Run a YouTube Channel

Though it is a social media of its own, it can be found in the Google search. To get the different audience and best Google search result you need it and that will bring traffic to your website.

27. Run a Podcast

In this modern days podcasts are more popular. In the podcast you can build a loyal group of audience.

28. Bring a Webinar

Sometimes bring a webinar to train your audience. In this way you will build trust among your audience and thus more traffic will come to your website.

29. Build an Email Newsletter

Use an email newsletter to promote your content through the website. In the email provide the link of your website where readers can read your web page. You can use MailChimp as your email newsletter

30. Open Account on StumbleUpon

StumbleUpon can promote your content easily. Through Stumble if you can collect more upvote you can reach hundred thousand people. Stumble upon sometimes offer paid advertising option.

31. Share Your Content on Reddit

Reddit never permit self-promotion. So you must hire someone to work for you. Remember one thing that you must submit quality content in the relevant subreddit. Otherwise, your content will be removed. It has also paid ads.

32. Sign up for (HARO)

HARO will provide you and email list. In this list journalist sometimes look sources for their stories. Apply the needed source related to your business.

33. Use AllTop

Use AllTop to bring more traffic to your website.

34. Reply to Your Commenters

If you reply to your commenters, they will be happy and thus you will build your trust and brand among the communities.

35. Answer on Q&A

Answer questions on Quora or Yahoo! Answers, and try to give the best answers related to questions and add links on your website.

36. Response to Your Post

Respond to your post to your popular articles to build more audience.

37. Conduct Interviews

When you will conduct interviews with the famous people, they will share that their audience and thus your website will be shared.

38. Build Network in Person

Try to participate networking event and talk with the person about your product and website.

39. Become Speaking Gig

Participating in the event as a speaker, you can talk about your business and about your website. Thus, you can build your own audience and brand which will bring more traffic to your website.

40. Apply Microformatting

Use Schema.org to format your site's data which may boost your chance of getting featured in Google's Knowledge Graph.

41. Offer in-Store motivations

Never forget your physical customers. Give them reasons to visit your website. Sometimes, offer discounts or cash voucher.

42. Publish a Press Release

Use media like PR Newswire or PRWeb to submit a press release related to your business event.

43. Submit a Product Review

On the net you will find so many products for review. Provide honest review which will build your brand image.

44. Mimic Your Competition

Find out what kind of strategies your competitors are using. If you want to compete, you try the best one.

45. Differentiate from Your Competition

Try something new from others. People will not go for the same thing. You need to reshape your product presenting it attractive ways.

46. Publish an eBook

Publish and eBook and build your email list by providing free copies to the audience. By this way you can get so many emails and now and then you can send your promotion through email and instantly they will visit your website after getting your mail.

47. Begins a Content Marketing Strategy

To drive more traffic to your website, begin by publishing high quality content on your webpage. Put keywords in it and through search engine traffic will come to visit your website.

How to Tap into Popular Traffic Sources

Fig 14 Auxiliary Sites

The fastest way to direct traffic onto your site is to tap into an already existing traffic flow. As shown in Fig.14, there are several places where this traffic flow can be tapped. These places include Facebook, YouTube, eBay, KSL, Craigslist, USfreeads, Etsy, Pinterest, and Amazon.

Facebook is the most popular site on the internet today with over 1 billion followers and still growing. You can tap into Facebook traffic flows by opening up a Facebook page. On your Facebook page, you can put some of your items for sale with links to your products website. You can find creative ways of engaging Facebook visitors to your site by offering freebies, inviting them to like your page, and actively engaging your followers with surprises, such as funny video clips, amazing offers, and new products. Once you get a follower on Facebook to like your page, that liking reflects on that follower's timeline which is visible to that follower's friends.

The best way to expose your page to Facebook fans is to go viral. How do you go viral? Simply create an amazing video or photo and followers of your page will share it with their friends, and these friends will share it with their friends, and friends' friends... ad infinitum – that is viral!

Other than Facebook, YouTube is becoming one of the most followed websites on the internet today. Have a funny video uploaded to your YouTube account, post the links to your website, Facebook page, and request followers to post the same on their website and also, email to their friends. This is another way to go viral.

Do you have an amazing knockdown offer that you auction on eBay? Yes, eBay is one of the most popular auction sites. You can offer some of your products at an amazingly low price, instead of offering them as freebies, and people will be competing to buy them. With a link to your website, this is a good way to tap into eBay traffic flows.

Buying an Already Existing Website or URL

One of the best ways to jumpstart your product sales are to buy a site that has similar products or has a SEO friendly URL. This would ensure that your product would gain instant exposure advantage since the new website or URL is already ranked in the search engines and already has traffic flows.

BUYING AND SELLING WEBSITES

- Should I create a website or buy one?

- Flippa.com
- Scriptlance
- Websitebroker.com

Fig 14b Places to buy websites

Fig.14b shows some of the places to buy an already existing website. If you can find a website to buy that meets your needs, it is a far better idea than building your own website. However, this depends on the cost-benefit analysis. Should you find that it is expensive to buy the website then you would just have to take the long route of building your own?

At scriptlance you can easily find coders who can develop a new website for you. Flippa is one of the leading places to buy already existing websites for sale.

Fig 14c Flippa

How to Outsource Your Common Tasks

Fig 15 Outsourcing common tasks

Online business requires a lot of varied skills and effort. Therefore, you can hardly do everything on your own. Common skills and tasks that you would require are outlined in Fig.14. Other tasks include optimizing your website so that it can easily be searchable (SEO), monitoring traffic flows, managing your online community, sending sales letters and emails, following up on leads, etc. You cannot afford to do all these alone, yet, it would be too expensive to employ each of these experts to do your tasks on a full time basis.

The best way to handle these tasks is to outsource them – yes, let others do it for you as independent contractors. The advantage of outsourcing to independent contractors is that you not only have a pool of experts, but you also pay for services rendered. You do not need to pay for annual leave, sick leave, personnel medical insurance, and so many other costs associated with hiring permanent staff.

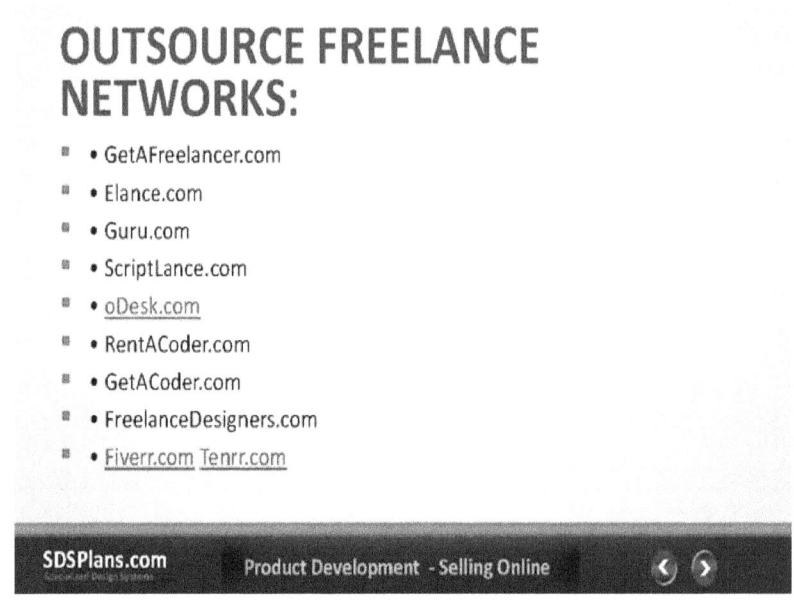

Fig 16 Freelance networks

How do you outsource your common tasks? There are various online sites to find freelancers who can do various tasks on your behalf. Fig.16 shows some of the popular outsourcing available to you.

Amongst these outsourcing sites, Elance and Upwork rank the highest. Each of the two sites operates professionally and provides an opportunity for you to get the best skilled contractors to do your work. However, there is a trade-off between choosing Elance and Upwork. One advantage of Elance over

Upwork is that Elance has an escrow account that allows both the contractor and client some degree of certainty. A client can deposit a certain amount of money which is usually an upfront payment or down payment into an escrow account and this money can only be released to the contractor by the client upon discharge of agreed terms. The client cannot withdraw this money without the consent of the contractor and neither can the contractor access the account. The other advantage of Elance over Upwork is the dispute resolution mechanism. Elance resolves disputes between the client and contractor while Upwork does not engage itself in dispute resolution. On the other hand, Upwork has one important advantage, and that is Upwork Team, which is basically software that remotely monitors what a contractor is doing on his computer. Upwork Team is applied for hourly payment contracts and which assures that a contractor bills you according to active hours worked. As Upwork Team captures the screen, keyboard taps, and mouse movements and also has an option for video capture. This ensures that a contractor cannot bill you for hours not worked. The second advantage of Upwork over Elance is that it has no minimum limit of what a contractor can bill you. Elance specifies a minimum limit of about $30 which discourages small tasks to be carried out on it, while Upwork allows as little as $1 and even less for an hourly rate.

How to Take Advantage from Untouched Online Traffic Sources.

For generating traffic, most of the people concentrate on the search engine Google. The main reason people choose to do this is it is found that 93% of online experiences begins with Google search, where Google has 80 global market shares. So, if you want to generate traffic, the Google search engine will be the best for you.

There are some other sources of traffic, which can bring a good number of traffic to your website if you can take advantage from them. You may think some lesser known alternative for online traffic. This will help you to find different sources and it will make you less dependable on Google. Following some strategies you can find some visitors and can take the traffic advantage for your website.

Blog Comments

Comment can help you build your brand, demonstrate your expertise and motivate others to visit your site. On the other hand, when you will leave a comment on another blog, the visitors will get the way to visit your website. Following some steps, you can bring more traffic by your comment.

Be First

Make yourself as the best bloggers in your industry and be the first to provide comment on the new blog. This will give you the more visibility as most of the commenters will come later and more likely many visitors will click on your site link.

Be Good

Try to make every comment helpful and valuable. Provide appropriate information. In this case, if you have reference link, provide that too with hard copy info. Keep an eye to other websites who use your articles in their sites. When you will find them, leave a thank for them in the forum. Certainly, never forget to answer comments on your own blog.

Email

Nowadays, email has become an unknown method to generate traffic with the influence of Google. That's why many underestimate email online traffic. By email, you can get a direct connection to your audience. The email owners might have social media account where they might share your link. That means one email may generate huge traffic.

By following tips and techniques, you can take advantage from your email traffic source.

Prepare a Bribe

If you provide quality content, many people will be happy to get your email list to get more of it. But if you provide bonuses for signing up, many people will be crowded to get it. Providing e-book or content upgrade, you can deliver an offer for your most popular post.

Add Signup Forms to Your Site

Adding sing up form you can get some list of emails. You can use SumoMe and OptinMonster for sign up.

Create a Welcome Email:

When someone will sign up to your subscription, send them and welcome email as a courtesy. While you will do this, send them product info and tell them to ask anything they need introducing your business. Certainly, it will make a difference. Along with these, there are other skills like writing killer subject in the email.

Image Sharing Sites

The Image has massive users who bring traffic to your sites. By the following examples you will understand.

- Instagram — 600 million users
- Pinterest — 150 million users
- Flickr — 122 million users
- Imgur — 150 million users
- Deviantart — 38 million users

You can easily understand that these sites can bring huge potential traffic to your websites. If the images are part of your content, you had better consider investing here. By following ways you can do this

Include a web link in your bio:

If you sign up to any website, add your website link in your bio. Even in every social platform you should use this. From your bio info the visitors will find you easily.

Use the tools at hand

Different websites have different kinds of tools to share images best possible ways. For instance, Flicker uses tags, Instagram uses hashtags. You should include these tools while sharing images.

Include links in posts

While you post your images, link your website too. In both places, try to use it in your description and in the image. You can use some text on your pics or put some watermarking.

Ask for backlinks

People search images in the flickers to make their own content. Adding a call to action to your images, you can put a backlink to your site. Uploading quality pictures you can make your content SEO list.

Document Sharing Sites

Like image documents also works the same way. You can share your documents on the Slideshare or other share. Slideshare has 70 million users like other image sharing sites.

How to Use Slideshare for Generating Traffic?

- Pick a trending topic — Find a most gossip topic or gather idea from your old blogs where you will find people's interest on the topics.
- Create an outline — Transform your blog content into slide just cutting additional description of your blog.
- Include keywords — Include Keywords to find your presentation in the search. Include your title, page number files and description.
- Use images — Including images, make your file more attractive
- Include a call to action — At the end of the slide include address and CTA. From where the reader will directly come to your site.

Besides Slideshare, you can post your slide documents in the following sites:

- Animoto
- Scribd
- Slideworld
- Slideboom

Include Your Email Signature:

Add your webpage link in your email signature. You may not like it. But think how many email you send every day? At least everyday more than dozen email we send. Your every single email is the tiny ambassador for your webpage. And in every moment it can inform the email user.

You need not add it manually. Rather, using app Wisestamp you can include it automatically.

How to Market Your Products Website

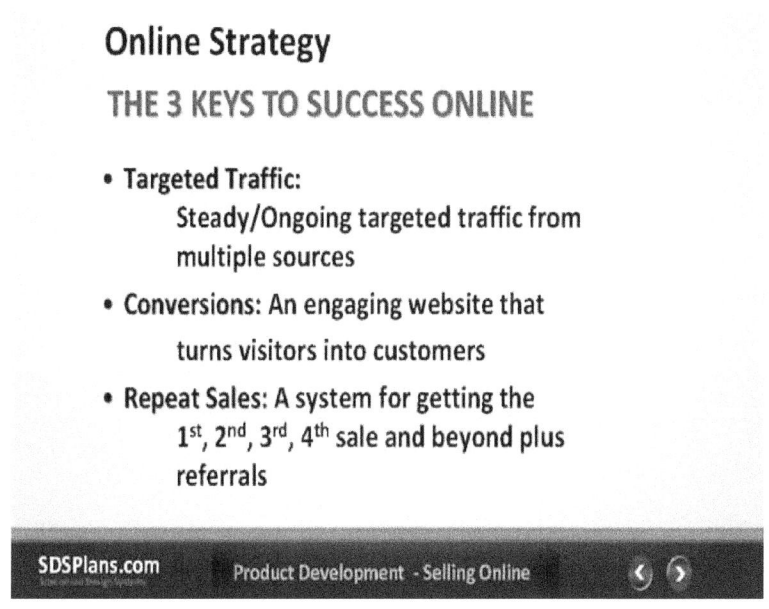

Fig 17 Online strategy

To market your products website, it requires clever strategies. Some of these strategies as outlined in Fig.17 include targeted traffic, conversions, and repeat sales.

Targeted Traffic

Targeted traffic is that traffic that flows from an already defined source. Before you start marketing your products website, you need to do some prior research to know what potential customers are looking for online, in terms of the keywords they use to search for your product and also the kind of sites they visit most.

There are various ways by which you can establish targeted traffic. These include:

- SEO Marketing
- Online Directories
- Auxiliary Sites
- Blogs and Forums

SEO Marketing

We briefly looked at SEO under 'How to generate traffic to your products website'. This was basically using the internal mechanisms, that is, optimizing your website for SEO purposes. However, you can also apply external mechanisms, which means using SEO on other websites to drive traffic to your site. This is what is called SEO Marketing.

Fig 18 SEO Marketing

As depicted by Fig. 18, some of the SEO Marketing tools include Press Releases, Articles, Videos, Slides, and photos.

Press Releases

A Press Release is a special statement that is geared towards providing factual information to the public about an organization's status, events, and activities such as an anniversary celebration, product launch, new product features, key staff hiring, key staff promotion, a new technological breakthrough, special offers, etc.

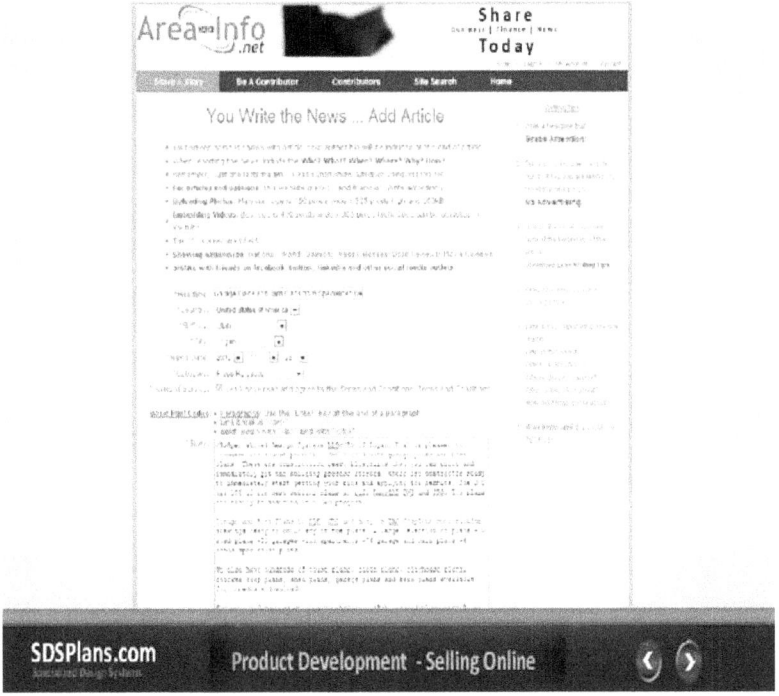

Fig 18a Area info PR site

A Press Release is a good way to subtly market your product without being overly loaded with a sales pitch. A Press Release needs to be SEO friendly in order for it to generate traffic.

There are various Press Release sites such as PR Web and Area-Info (shown in Fig.18a) with huge traffic flows that can easily direct traffic to your products website.

SEO Articles

Articles have of late taken a huge chunk of online marketing. People seem to be fatigued by billions of bombarding advertisements, such that they avoid pop ups by employing pop up blockers and the like. Therefore, a subtle advertisement where a prospective customer is persuaded through an informative yet, professional article, is the best way to go.

A SEO article is different from an ordinary informative article in the sense that it has SEO keywords that attract traffic to it. Once the traffic is attracted to it, it is then deflected back to your products website. For this deflection to succeed, the article must be put in such a persuasive and professional manner that would inspire readers to follow links outlined in it, of which these links leads to various pages or segments of your products page.

You can easily outsource writing of these SEO articles to outsourcing sites such as Upwork, Elance, and Freelancer. You can either post these articles yourself to online article directories or let your contractor easily do it for you.

Some of the common online article directories include ezine articles (shown in Fig.19), linkvana, squidoo lens, ehow, etc.

Fig 19 Ezine

Videos

They say a picture speaks a thousand words. Well, what about a motion of hundreds to thousands of pictures, accompanied by spoken and written words? Yes, that's video and the a million words it is capable of communicating.

There are billions of text contents to read online. This can bring heavy fatigue on readers. To have an alternative mode of delivery that can relieve this fatigue and drive your point home fast, you need to use the power of video.

Spend a little time, effort, and money to make up a video that describes your product, its features, its usage, and how to get it and you will have tapped a huge market.

19a types of videos to create

Luckily, if you are not a professional in this, you can get a professional contractor, from the plenty of outsourcing sites available, to do a video for you.

Once you have completely done your video, simply create a free YouTube account, and upload it. This has the capability of reaching traffic of over a billion visitors. To enhance this exposure, you can embed the same video on your products' website and attach links to various other auxiliary sites such as Facebook, Twitter, LinkedIn, Pinterest, Stumble Upon, and so many others.

Slides

Do you ever hear talk of PowerPoint online? Yes, there are various sites online such as Slide Share that enables slide presentation. The goodness of slide presentation is that it is a sleek way of presenting content within a limited space.

On sites such as Slide Share (shown in Fig.19a), you only need to upload your content and the content will be converted into a slide. Slide Share is such a site that receives a huge traffic flow, which you can easily redirect to your products website.

19a Slide Share

Wondering how to do it? You need not worry, because there are plenty of contractors on outsourcing sites who are ready to do it for you at extremely affordable rates.

Photos

Photos are a good way to capture attention. A photo easily represents information at a glance. Having a photo that is SEO friendly, which means having a caption and 'alt' (alternative text to photo), that is search engine optimized accompanied by appropriate links, can easily drive traffic to your site.

You not only need to place interesting and professionally done photos on your products site, but you also need to place such photos on sites likeFacebook, Pinterest, Flickr, stumble upon, Tumblr, LinkedIn, etc. This would grant your products page maximum exposure.

Online Directories

Fig 20 Online Directory

There are various online directories where you can register your products website and products. You can also post articles on these online directories.

Some of the popular online directories include yellow pages and craigslist. You can also use article directories such as ezine articles, linkvana, squidoo lens, EHow, etc. Other online directories are listed in Fig.20.

Auxiliary Sites

We had previously talked about auxiliary sites such as Facebook, Twitter, YouTube, etc. These sites are good for you to embed links to your products website.

Online stores are also a good way to market your products website. You simply need to take a sample of your products and post them on online stores such as Amazon, eBay, Etsy, KSL, and others with links to your products website. This is so potential customers can not only buy from such sites, but also can click on the product's link which leads them to your website.

Blogs and Forums

Blogs and forums are a good place to market your products website. You would need to check for blogs and forums that focus on products similar to your own or touching on the industry to which your respective products belong to. Give comments on such blogs and forums with links pointing to your product's website.

You can also establish your own blogs as part of either your website or as independent blog or both. This would improve on interactions with both existing and potential customers.

Conversions

However nice your products site is, if it can't convert visitors into customers, repeat customers and referrals, then it is not such an asset. What brings about site conversion? There are several factors that facilitate conversion:

- Site Mechanics
- Marketing Campaigns
- Traffic flows

Site Mechanics

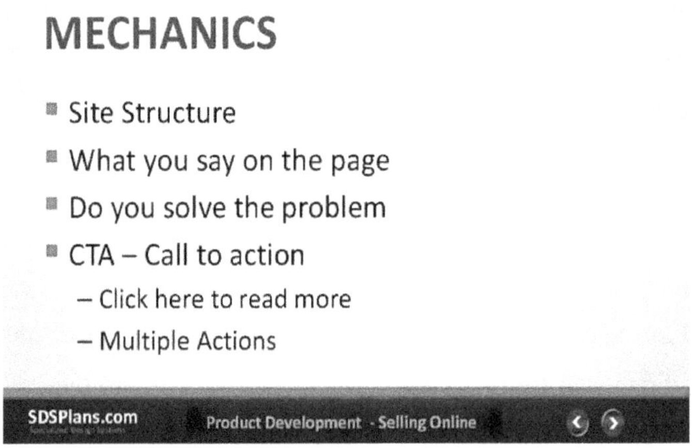

Fig 21 Site Mechanics

Site mechanics refers to how your site is designed, starting from the coding, content display, content language, and content value. Fig.21 shows some of the important consideration in the site mechanics.

Site Structure

Your products site should be structured in such a manner that not only optimizes on search ability, but also optimizes on navigability. The site should be easy to use and easy to navigate from one page to another to and from.

Content Value

The content you put on your site should not only describe what you say, but also how you say it. What you say must be such that it is factual. How you say it, concerns it with how you express your language and answers the following questions; is your language easy to understand? Is your language clear and concise? Is your language courteous and respectful? All these add to content value, which would inspire potential customers.

Do You Solve the Problem?

There is no need to spend your time and effort deriving tons of content that is irrelevant to the potential customers' needs. Your content and the website as a whole must solve the problem that the potential customer is seeking solutions to.

Call to Action – CTA

Have you excited the potential customer enough to press the 'BUY BUTTON'? You must create the need and urgency in the potential customer's psychology so that the customer can feel how inevitable it is to buy the item.

Online Marketing Campaigns

Online marketing campaigns can be carried out through various means that include:

- Email Marketing
- Adverts
- Use of classified ads
- Use of social media
- Placing your products on online stores
- Weekly promotion campaigns

Email Marketing

Fig 22 Email marketing

Email is one of the easiest ways to market your products. Once you have emails of customers and potential customers, then it is easy to make sales promotions through their emails.

There are various online facilities that can help you manage your email marketing campaigns. One of these tools is Call Loop.

Fig 23 Call Loop

Fig.23 depicts Call Loop facility. Call Loop helps you to manage your email campaigns by making it easy to create instant and periodic email newsletters and post them automatically to the listed emails. Call Loop also has SMS text facility that helps you send mass SMS automatically to listed mobile phone numbers.

Advertising

Advertising is a popular means of advertising online due to the ease, flexibility, and affordability of online adverts. Online adverts, unlike outdoor or radio and TV adverts, are extremely flexible in terms of budget. You can have adverts for as low as $5 or even free!

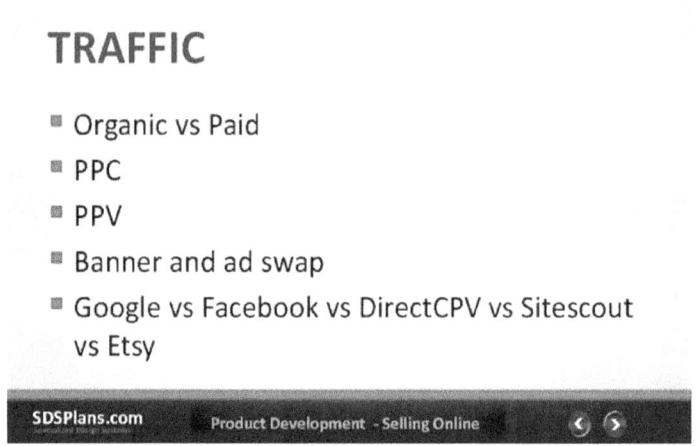

Fig 24 Traffic

Fig.24 shows the various types of sources of traffic. Organic traffic is one that arises out of visitors own effort to arrive at your site. Paid traffic is one that is directed to your site through advertisement. This paid traffic can be derived from PPC (Pay Per Click) or PPV (Pay Per View). PPC is a mode of payment whereby you pay per every click on the posted advert. Therefore, the click becomes the recognition that the advert has attained its objective. PPV is a mode of payment whereby you pay per every view of a posted advert irrespective of whether the advert is clicked on or not. PPV is generally cheaper than PPC, but with a lower conversation rate (that is, turning visitors into customers).

Fig 25 DirectCPV

There are various online advertisement companies including Google, Facebook, DirectCPV, Sitescount and Etsy. Each of these advertisement companies has its advantages and disadvantages. Google is so far the most expensive of them all, and its adverts have the widest reach. Facebook has the second widest reach. However, Facebook allows you to make adverts for as low as $5.

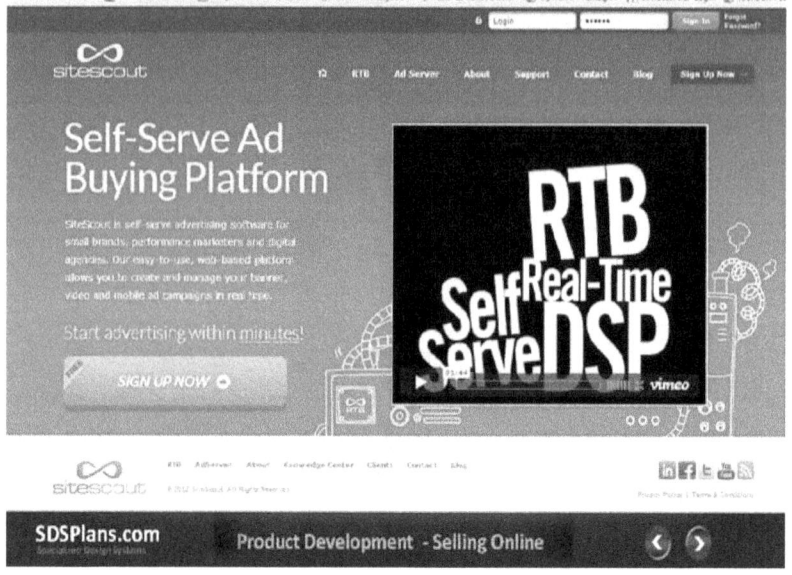

Fig 26 Sitescount

Use of Classified Ads

There are various sites that provide space for classified ads either free or at a small fee depending on the type and extend of service that you require.

Some of these classified ads sites include:

- KSL
- USFreeAds
- Fiverr
- Craigslist
- Backpage
- Quikr
- Gumtree
- Ebay classifieds

- inetgiant
- olx.com
- oodle
- adpost
- salespider
- aslandpro
- Yakaz
- Wiju.com
- Sell.com
- Pennysaverusa
- hooblyClaz
- geebo

Fig 27 KSL

KSL.com allows you to post classified ads. KSL is one of the largest classified ads site and has millions of visitors. Placing your ad on KSL can bring a huge traffic to your products site where customers can buy. USFreeAds is another place to put your classified ads. For only $6 per month subscription, you can have plenty of ads on USFreeAds, which will generate lots of traffic to your products site leading to increased sales.

Use of Social Media

- Social media has billions of members. The three leading social media sites to place your adverts are:
- Facebook
- Twitter
- Pinterest

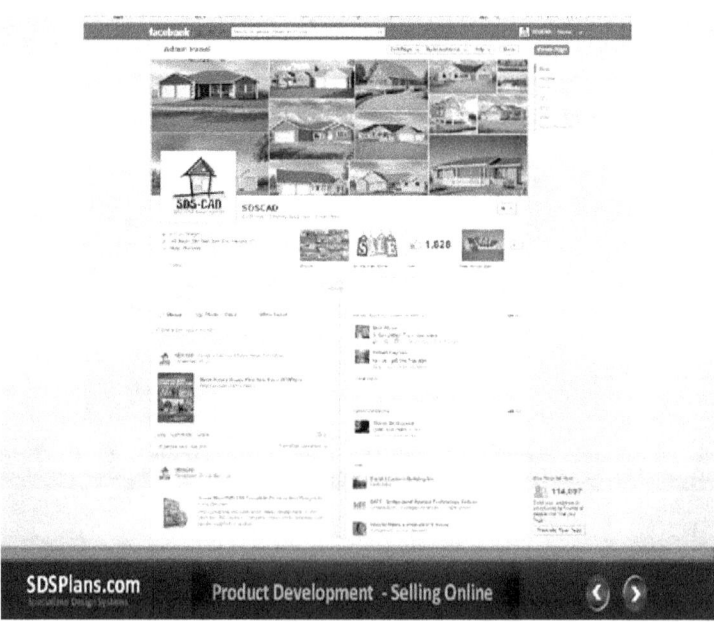

Fig 28 Facebook

You can easily open up a Facebook page like the one shown in Fig.28, where you can arrange your products and put links to your site where customers can buy the products. This is the cheapest way of generating traffic from Facebook into your products site.

Fig 29 Twitter

Twitter is another place to put up your adverts. Although twitter is so limited in its usage, such that it mainly allows text, you can create a text with a link and tweet it which works like a massive online 'SMS'. The good thing about twitter is that you can easily integrate it into your own website as shown in in Fig.29 above.

Pinterest is such a wonderful social media where you can display your photos just as you would do with a classified ad. However, unlike classified ads, there is no provision for you to quote prices and put the 'buy' button that would lead to shopping cart. Therefore, you can put photos of your products with links to your respective products page as shown in Fig.30.

Fig 30 Pinterest

Placing Your Products on Online Stores

One other way to market your products is to place them on online stores. There are various major online stores whose suitability depends on your nature of product. The following are some of the major stores online:

- Amazon
- EBay
- etsy
- clickbank

Both Amazon and eBay sells virtually every kind of product.

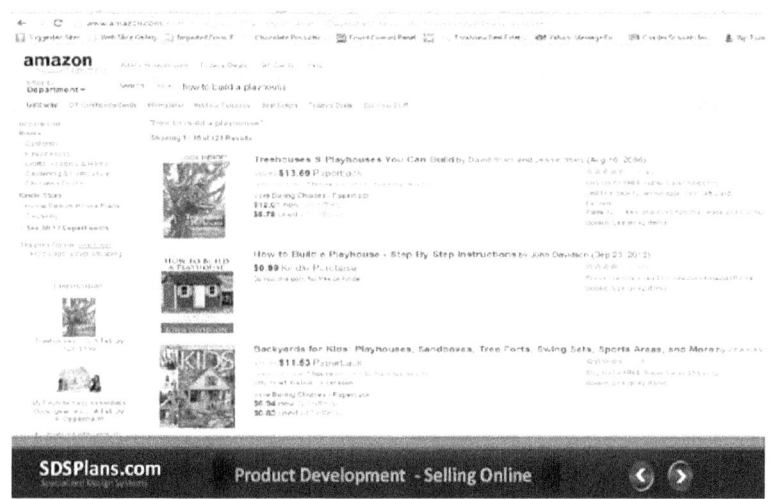

Fig 31 Amazon

Amazon

Amazon is the world's largest online store that deals with virtually every kind of product. Amazon sells millions of items a day and thus has an extremely huge traffic flow. Furthermore, other than being able to sell on Amazon, it also gives you an opportunity to have backlinks to your products page and even provides an opportunity for a free press release about your product.

Ebay

EBay is the leading competitor of Amazon and equally receives huge traffic and has hundreds of thousands of products on its online store. This makes it an important market to place your products for sale and also receive back links to your products website.

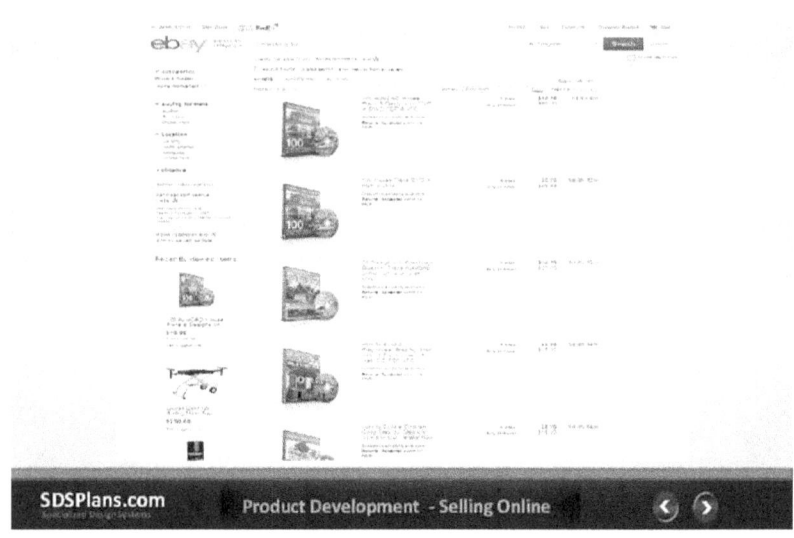

Fig 32 EBay Store

Clickbank

Clickbank is one of the largest online affiliate sites today. It has hundreds of thousands of affiliates who market products on its site. Other than displaying your products on Clickbank, most affiliates have their own websites which display your products on them. This acts like a free advert for your products. Clickbank is also a good source of backlinks to your products website.

Etsy

Etsy is a good site for selling products online. Etsy is ideal for small items, especially handicrafts and household items. At etsy, you only need to pay about $0.2 per item plus about 3% of sales made. The other great advantage of etsy is that you can pay to have your product rank high in addition to having your own shopping cart.

Fig 33 Etsy

Weekly Promotional Campaigns

Marketing, though easy to do, requires a high level of frequency. To maintain and improve your products' online presence, you need to have a weekly promotional campaign as outlined in Fig.34. This weekly promotional campaign would not only ensure that there is increased traffic flow, continued exposure of your products online, but also improved search engine ranking which would further expose your products website to more traffic flow.

WEEKLY PROMOTION METHOD

- Write a press release or article and submit
- Turn it into a Slide Show and submit
- Turn it into a video and submit
- Post on my Blog, Facebook, Twitter
- Weekly Newsletter or Blog Summery to List
- Bookmark, Ping

SDSPlans.com   Product Development - Selling Online

Fig 34 Schedule of weekly promotions

Automated Promotion

We have looked at all the outlined methods of promoting your products. However, it is not so easy to promote your website onto dozens of available media, such as video media and social media, on weekly basis without the help of automation.

As indicated by Fig.35, there are two good facilities for automating weekly promotions; OnlyWire and OneLoad.

OnlyWire is a social media automating facility whereby you put up your promotion that you expect to go to social media, and it will automatically post on all your existing social media such as Facebook, Twitter, LinkedIn, etc.

OneLoad is a video sharing automating facility whereby you upload your promotional video on it and it automatically posts the video on all leading Video Channels and sites.

Fig 35 Onlywire and oneload

With these two automating facilities, you can save loads of time, effort and money.

Conclusion

Developing products and selling them online has become not only the most effective and efficient way of doing business, but also the ultimate means of reaching billions of potential customers worldwide. Establishing your online presence can be, at times, a cumbersome and expensive endeavor if not well informed and organized. This book provides the much-needed practical information and guidelines that can enable you to maximize benefits out of your product and business endeavor. Yet, the book alone cannot satisfy all the modes of communication that can enable you to have an all-round perspective. You need to attend workshops and seminars such as those conducted by John Davidson or watch his highly educative and inspirational videos. Visiting some of his sites such as http://sdsplans.com would be the best way of understanding how he has managed to be a successful online entrepreneur, and from which source the inspiration to write this book emanates.

About the Author

John Davidson is an online products development guru who has been developing and selling products online since the year 2000. John is an accomplished writer, trainer and highly successful guest speaker conducting various educational seminars pertaining to his pet subject – online business development. As a writer, John has published over 1,200 books and sold over 1,000,000 copies of them online.

John is an accomplished Architectural draftsman who has successfully utilized the power of eCommerce to sell thousands of architectural plans worldwide. As an internet business entrepreneur, John runs over 200 websites managed under his company – Specialized Design Systems which comprises of full-time staff and freelancers located across the globe.

As an internet techpreneur, John has developed dozens of mobile apps with over 1,000,000 downloads so far. Before venturing into business online, John has been drawing homes, barns, and garages since 1984. He has drawn over 500 homes and over 1000 garages and barns thanks to his family drafting business Specialized Design Systems.

On one of his architectural design websites, http://housecabin.com has over 100 full house and cabin plans available for easy download for as low as $1 each. John has been selling affordable digital plans online for over 15 years. Check out more of his plans at http://sdsplans.com which is Specialized Designs Systems LLC plan website.

John's newest project is a series of nonfiction children's books about animals geared towards first time or young readers the website is http://AmazingAnimalBooks.com

This book was developed from a lecture John gave at the Cache Business Resource Centers Business Summit.

Check out some of the other JD-Biz Publishing books

<u>Gardening Series on Amazon</u>

Health Learning Series

Country Life Books

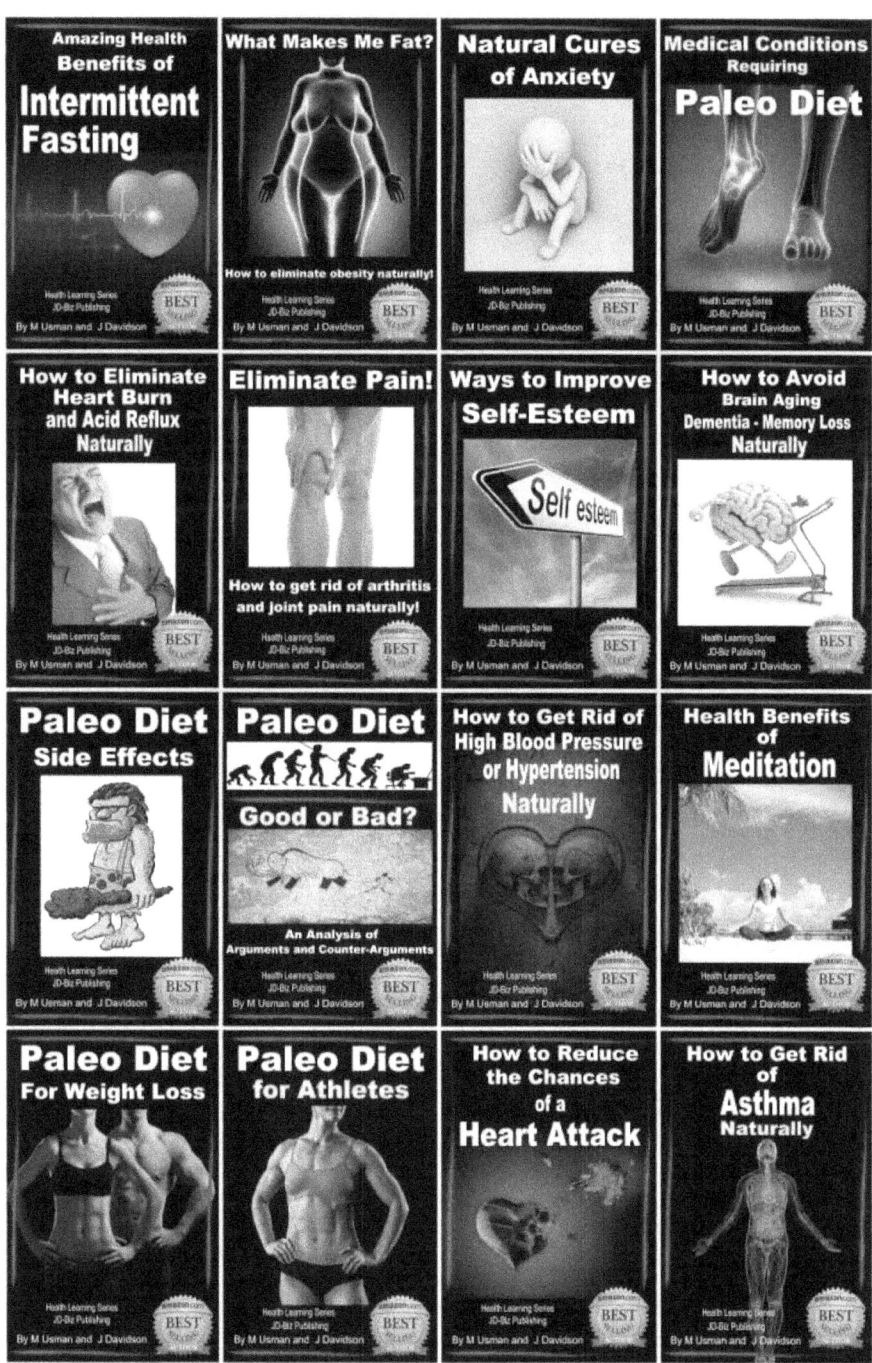

Amazing Animal Book Series

Learn To Draw Series

How to Build and Plan Books

Entrepreneur Book Series

Our books are available at

1. Amazon.com

2. Barnes and Noble

3. Itunes

4. Kobo

5. Smashwords

6. Google Play Books

Download Free Books!
http://MendonCottageBooks.com

Publisher

JD-Biz Corp

P O Box 374

Mendon, Utah 84325

http://www.jd-biz.com/

Mendon Cottage Books
P O Box 374, Mendon Utah 84325